"If you have the gift, this book will show you how to use it."
—Victoria Wisdom, Literary Agent, Becsey, Wisdom & Kalajian

"Contains chapter and verse on all aspects of screenwriting, and addresses every key and fundamental principle from how far to indent dialogue to how to speak to the agent's assistant."
—Screenwrite Now!

*"Offers all the essential information in one neat, script-sized volume....
New screenwriters will find* The Screenwriter's Bible *invaluable; experienced screenwriters will find it an excellent addition to their reference shelf."*
—Hollywood Scriptwriter

*"Delivers more in 195 pages than can be found in several screenwriting books.
A true gem that measures up to its title."*
—Writer's Connection

"...Easy to read and surprisingly broad in its coverage."
—New York Screenwriter

"The formatter alone is worth the price of the book."
—Melissa Jones, Hollywood Story Analyst

"Good, common sense. Sets up practical guidelines without encroaching on the writer's creativity. Easy to follow—feels like a workbook that will be used and not just read. The author is encouraging, but reminds the writer of the realities of the business."
—Candace Monteiro, Co-owner, Monteiro Rose Agency

"Just what the script doctor ordered . . . a 'must have' reference tool for new and experienced screenwriters. Straight-forward, to the point, and accurate."
—Wisconsin Screenwriter's Forum

The Bible provides clear answers to crucial questions

- How do I find an agent in today's difficult marketplace?

- How do I sell my script if I don't have an agent?

- How do I break into Hollywood when I live in Peoria?

- How do I summon my Muse and increase my creativity energy?

- What is the Character/Action Grid and what makes it so fast and effective in evaluating and revising my work?

- What twelve common formatting mistakes turn off agents and readers?

- What are the tricks to effective scene construction and transition?

- How do I write a query letter that will get my script read?

- How do I build a winning, compelling pitch? What are the unwritten rules?

- Where is Hollywood's *back door* and how do I get through it?

- How do I break into television and the cable markets?

- What are the ten keys to creating captivating characters?

- What basic plot paradigms do virtually all stories conform to?

- What writing opportunities are often overlooked by screenwriters?

- What is *high concept* and how can I use it to sell my screenplay?

- Where can I find a clear writing process that will motivate me to finish my script?

- How can I add dimension, depth, and emotion to virtually any story?

- What are the ten tools every writer needs (and few have) before approaching the market?

- Where can I find a list of contests, software, help lines, and other resources?

- What is the single most important key to writing great dialogue?

- Where can a new writer find an inexpensive critique of his or her script?

- How does Hollywood really work?

It's all in *The Bible*

THE SCREENWRITER'S bible

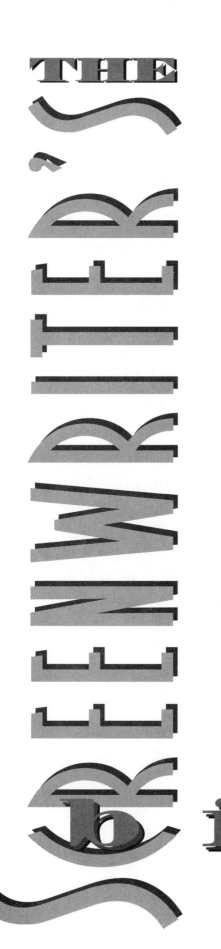

THE SCREENWRITER'S

Bible

A COMPLETE GUIDE TO WRITING, FORMATTING, AND SELLING YOUR SCRIPT

REVISED EDITION

BY DAVID TROTTIER

SILMAN-JAMES PRESS
Los Angeles

Kerry Cox, *Bed of Lies* query letter, © 1993 *The Hollywood Scriptwriter*, All Rights Reserved. Reprinted courtesy *The Hollywood Scriptwriter*.

Joni Sensel, Excerpts from "More Queries From Hell" and *The Wizard of Oz* query letter, © 1993 Northwest Screenwriter, All Rights Reserved. Reprinted courtesy Joni Sensel and Northwest Screenwriter.

Karen Mitura, *Heart of Silence* query letter, © 1993 Forum Publishing. Reprinted courtesy Karen Mitura and the Screenwriter's FORUM.

Jeff Warshaw, *The Silk Maze* query letter, © Jeff Warshaw. Reprinted courtesy the author.

Library of Congress Cataloging-in-Publication Data

Trottier, David.
The screenwriter's bible : a complete guide to writing, formatting, and selling your script / by David Trottier.
p. cm.
Orginally published: Anaheim, CA : Screenwriting Center, c1994.
Includes bibliographical references and index.
1. Motion picture authorship. 2. Television authorship.
I. Title.
PN1996.T76   808.2'3--dc20   95-31297

ISBN: 1-879505-26-6

Cover design by Heidi Frieder

Printed in the United States of America.

SILMAN-JAMES PRESS
1181 Angelo Drive
Beverly Hills, CA 90210
FAX (310) 271-7243

Dedicated to the developing screenwriter
and to students and clients
who have inspired me with their dedication and creative vision.

A special thanks to three writers
who years ago encouraged me to write:
Greg Alt, Don Moriarty, and Stephen J. Stirling

Contents

How to use *The Bible*

I have spent eight years working with aspiring writers. Throughout this period, I have realized that there are core principles and techniques that help writers get off to a fast start. In this volume, I help you begin the journey and guide you along the way. Not that you won't need help and encouragement from others—you will—but that every aspect of screenwriting is covered in this work. That's why I call it *The Screenwriter's Bible*.

There are five guidebooks or sections in *The Bible*. Each book is self-contained and can be read independently of the others. In addition, each can be used as a handy reference. You will find yourself turning to *The Bible* again and again. Most writers, regardless of experience, will benefit from a thorough reading of all five books. Here's a helpful insight into each book or section.

- *Book I: How to Write a Screenplay* is based on my cassette series of the same name, which won the Best Instructional Audio Cassettes Award from The Screenwriter's FORUM. My hope is that you'll find it a concise and clear presentation of screenwriting essentials. Use it as a textbook, or as a refresher when you're stuck. Books I and III can be used concurrently as you write your script. In fact, Book I will occasionally refer you to Book III (actually a *work*book) at appropriate junctures.

- *Book II: Correct Format for Screenplays & Teleplays* has been through five editions (and several printings) and has helped thousands correctly format their spec scripts. This new, sixth edition not only provides crucial information, but teaches something of screenwriting itself. Even if you have a complete knowledge of formatting, reading this book will improve your writing style. In addition to a complete index at the end, the text itself is cross-referenced throughout.

- *Book III: 7 Steps to a Stunning Script* is a workbook that takes you step by step through the writing process. The first step deals with creativity, "summoning your Muse," and overcoming blocks. The other six steps include the pre-writing, writing, and revision phases.

- *Book IV: How to Sell Your Script* presents a detailed marketing plan that takes the mystery out of selling to Hollywood and to the many other screenwriting markets. The plan is comprehensive as well as specific. With it, you'll be able to target your market with effective sales strategies. How I wish I had it so many years ago!

- Finally, *Book V: Resources and Index* lists over 100 screenwriting resources that you can use from the moment your idea is born to the consummation of a deal. The general index at the end will help you find the topics you want in an instant.

The Screenwriter's Bible is sold with the understanding that neither the publisher nor the author are engaged in rendering legal advice. If legal assistance is required, the services of an entertainment attorney or other professional should be sought.

I invite you to share with me your reactions to *The Bible* and hope it becomes a help and a guide to your personal writing success. I wish you the best.

David Trottier
Irvine, California
Autumn, 1995

ABOUT THE NEW, REVISED EDITION

This *Revised Edition* updates and expands the information of the first edition, with particular attention paid to Books II, IV, and V. The general index has been expanded to facilitate referencing.

D.T. 1995

HOW TO WRITE A SCREENPLAY

BOOK I

A Primer

How stories work

THE NEXT GREAT SCREENWRITER

You may have heard that breaking into the movie business is tough. It is.

However, if you write a script that features a character who has a clear and specific goal, where there is strong opposition to that goal leading to a crisis and an emotionally satisfying ending, your script will automatically find itself in the upper five percent. Few would-be writers have mastered even the basics of screenwriting. And most screenplays fail on the above criteria alone.

Now if your script also presents a well-crafted story with a strong story concept and an original character people can sympathize with, there are agents and producers awaiting the advent of the next great screenwriter.

You can be that next great screenwriter. You'll have to work, learn your craft, and develop discipline. You'll need to apply the fine art of pleasant persistence. And there are going to be disappointments. But you can do it! Now stop for just a moment, buck up, and say that to yourself.

Everyone begins the same. Everyone writes one or more feature-length scripts of about 120 pages. Even if you want to write for television, your best entrance is with a feature script that you can use as a sample. Book I is designed to help you write that one spec script that's going to get you noticed.

What is a spec script? It's the script you're writing now on the speculation that some-one will buy it later. (Book II will help you with formatting and style. Book III gives you specific direction in the actual writing of the script. Book IV helps you sell it. And Book V provides support.)

THE STRENGTH OF THE SCREENPLAY FORM

As the next great screenwriter, you're obviously going to write a screenplay. A screen-play differs from a stageplay or novel.

A novel may describe a character's thoughts and feelings page after page. It's a great medium for internal conflict. A stageplay is almost exclusively verbal. Soap operas and sitcoms fit into this category. A movie is primarily visual. Yes, it will contain dialogue. It may even deal with internal things. But it is primarily a visual medium that requires visual writing. I have never read a "first screenplay" that did not have too much dia-logue and too little action. You may have that same common tendency to tell rather than show.

For example, picture a **stageplay** where a babysitter cuts paper dolls with her scissors. The children are upstairs playing. From the other side of the room, a robber enters. He approaches her with a knife. Just in time, she turns and stabs him with the scis-sors. Not particularly exciting. In an actual stageplay, these people would probably talk to each other for ten minutes before the physical confrontation, because the conflict in a stageplay comes out in dialogue. That's the strength of the stageplay form.

A **novel** may focus on the thoughts and feelings of each character. That's the strength of the novel form—inner conflict. The babysitter is contemplating suicide. And this is the robber's first job. He's not sure he can go through with it.

However, a **screenplay** will focus on the visual aspects of the scene. The scissors pen-etrate one of the paper dolls. The doorknob slowly turns. The babysitter doesn't no-tice. Outside, the dog barks, but the kids upstairs are so noisy that she doesn't hear the dog. A figure slides in through the shadows. His knife fills the screen. He moves to-ward her. The dog barks louder. The intruder inches closer. But she is completely ab-sorbed in cutting paper dolls. He looms over her. His knife goes up. The dog barks louder still. She suddenly becomes aware, turns, and impales the man with the scissors. He falls. His legs twitch and finally become still. She drops the scissors and screams.

The focus here is on the action—the drama—because movies are primarily visual. Yes, there are notable exceptions, but you are wise to use the strength of the medium for which you have chosen to write. Inner conflict is great, dialogue is important to bring out interpersonal conflict, but make your screenplay visually powerful. *Showing* through action usually works better than *telling* with dialogue.

THE IMPORTANCE OF BEING STRUCTURED

Your screenplay must be well structured because the director and other collaborators are going to take your work of art and make it their own—you want the story to survive. This is one reason William Goldman emphasized in his book *Adventures in the Screen Trade* that "screenplays are structure."

Art is a union of form and content, whether it's a painting, a vase of flowers, a rock ballad, or your story. Accordingly, the *content* of your story requires a dramatic structure or *form* to give it shape. Structure is the skeleton on which you hang the meat of your story. And without that skeletal framework, your story content falls flat like a blob of jelly, incapable of forward movement.

Most beginning writers just begin writing without any thought of story structure—where it's going or how it will end. Soon, writer's block sets in. One of your first writing steps will be to construct a skeleton, a structural model. Let's discuss that basic model.

Aristotle was right

Aristotle wrote in his *Poetics* that all drama (and that includes comedy, since comedy is drama in disguise) has a beginning, a middle, and an end. You've heard this before. Traditionally, the beginning is about 25% of the story, the middle is approximately 50%, and the end is about 25%. This is the basic three-act structure. If you like to think in terms of four acts, then Act 1 is the beginning, Acts 2 and 3 are the middle, and Act 4 is the end.

Since a screenplay is about 120 pages, the beginning is usually the first 15-30 pages. The middle is the next 60 pages or so, and the end is the last 10-30 pages. Obviously, the exact length can vary, but the middle is the biggest section.

All great screenplays have a beginning, a middle, and an end. In the beginning, you set up your story, get the reader's attention, and establish the situation. During the middle, you complicate matters and develop the conflict that rises to a crisis. In the end, you conclude the story and resolve the conflict. This is the payoff for the reader, for the audience, and for you. Put your hero in the proverbial tree, throw rocks at her, and get her out. Boy meets girl, boy loses girl and tries to get her back again, boy gets girl. Beginning, middle, and end.

What about DOA? It opens with the ending. Granted, it opens with the end of the central character's life, but not with the end of the story. What is this story really about? It is not about his death, it's about who killed him. The dramatic premise is this: Can he find his killer before he dies? The story ends when he finds his killer. This is just a creative way of using the basic model.

In BACK TO THE FUTURE, the beginning takes place in 1985, the middle in 1955, and the end in 1985 again. A very simple overall framework.

Twists and Turns

How do you get from the beginning to the middle and from the middle to the end? Turning points. They are also called transition points, action points, plot points, and character crossroads. Turning points are the twists and turns of the story. They are the important events that complicate or even reverse the action, such as cliffhangers, revelations, and crises. Structure is the organization of these events into a story.

There may be dozens of turning points in your story, but the two that facilitate the transition from act to act are key to your story's success. The first big turning point ends Act 1 and moves the reader (and the audience) to Act 2. It could be called the *Big Event* because it is usually a "big event" that dramatically affects the central character's life.

The second major turning point moves the reader into Act 3 and the final showdown. This is the *Crisis*. Of all the crises in your story, this is the one that forces the central character to take the last final action, or series of actions, to resolve the story. Let's look at some examples.

In CHINATOWN, detective Jake Gittes deals with extramarital affairs. A woman claiming she is Mrs. Mulwray hires him to spy on her husband. So he takes some photographs of her husband with a girl. These are published in the *L.A. Times*, and his job is done. He celebrates at a barber shop, where he hears a dirty joke. Cheerfully, he returns to his office and tells his buddies the joke. He doesn't see the beautiful woman standing behind him. The tension increases as Jake tells his joke because we know he's going to be embarrassed when he finally notices the woman. Jake tells the joke, gives the punch line, and turns. Surprise. The woman informs him that her name is Mrs. Mulwray and that she never hired him to spy on her husband, and now she's suing him. He's been embarrassed a second time. The first embarrassment foreshadowed the second. There's a beginning, middle, and end in this scene.

Is this not a big event in Jake's life? Jake has big problems now. If this is the *real* Mrs. Mulwray, who was the *first* Mrs. Mulwray? Who set him up and why? And how is he going to save his reputation?

Steven Spielberg said that, in the best stories, someone loses control of his/her life and must regain it. The Big Event causes that loss of control. In GHOST, the Big Event is the murder of Patrick Swayze. In JUNIOR, Arnold Swartzenegger gets pregnant.

Now let's look at an example of the Crisis, or second major turning point, the one that moves us from the middle to the end. In E.T. it is the moment when E.T. is dying, and the men converge on the house. Everything looks bleak. It is the moment when it looks least likely that E.T. will ever get home. This is the Crisis. What follows is the last, final struggle to get home. You have a similar low point in THELMA & LOUISE. How will they ever escape the law now?

In SLEEPLESS IN SEATTLE, you feel pretty low when Meg Ryan announces that Tom Hanks is history and that she's finally decided to marry Walter. You feel even lower when you see the physical distance between the building she's dining in and the Empire State building Tom Hanks is headed for.

In the PURPLE ROSE OF CAIRO, Cecilia has a crummy life, a crummy husband, a crummy job, and lives during the Great Depression. For relief, she goes to the local theater where this week THE PURPLE ROSE OF CAIRO is playing. She's seen it four times already, and at the fifth showing, one of the fictitious characters in the movie notices her in the audience and walks right off the screen and into Cecilia's life. The Big Event—right?

The Big Event is the clincher in setting up your audience. They're now prepared for the long haul through the second and third acts. They want to know what happens next.

Let's take a closer look at this movie, THE PURPLE ROSE OF CAIRO. In the beginning, we are introduced to reality (Cecilia's husband and life) and then to fantasy (the fictitious character and movies in general). So what will happen in the middle? Can you guess? We'll have a rising conflict; in this case, fantasy vs. reality. This conflict will build to the Crisis. What's the Crisis going to be? It's when Cecilia has to choose between her husband (reality) and the fictitious character (fantasy).

The Crisis in this film is not just a low point but an event that forces the central character to make a crucial decision. Once she decides, then she can move into the final act, the Showdown (or climax) and resolution of the story.

In ALIENS, the Crisis is precipitated when the little girl is kidnapped by the alien creatures, and the planet is about to explode. Sigourney Weaver must make a crucial, life-or-death decision. Will she abandon the planet and save herself? Or will she return for the little girl? She demonstrates her choice by turning on her flame thrower.

CASABLANCA: The Big Event, which seems subtle enough, is when Ilsa enters Rick's place and says, "Play it, Sam." Sam tells her she's bad luck to Rick but plays "As Time Goes By" anyway. Then Rick enters and tells Sam, "I thought I told you never to play that song." Then Rick sees Ilsa. Obviously, there's a lot of history between these two people.

The Crisis in CASABLANCA occurs as follows: Ilsa must get the Letters of Transit from Rick. It's the only way she and her husband, Victor Laslow, can escape from the Nazis. One night, Rick returns to his room, and Ilsa is waiting for him. She pleads with him, but he will not give her the Letters of Transit. Finally, she pulls a gun on him. He says, "Go ahead and shoot, you'll be doing me a favor." Will Ilsa shoot him? That's her personal crisis in this story.

She can't and Rick realizes that she must still love him. They have their moment together and then Ilsa says that she can never leave Rick again. "I don't know what's right any longer. You have to decide for both of us, for all of us." Ilsa turns the responsibility over to Rick because he is the central character, and as such he should be the most active person in Act 3. Rick accepts by saying, "All right, I will." Here, Rick agrees to make the crucial decision about whom will benefit from the Letters of Transit. The rest of the story—the end, the final act—is the unfolding of Rick's decision.

Several years ago, I discovered the perfect drama: Dickens' *A Christmas Carol*. We are first introduced to Scrooge, Tiny Tim, Bob Cratchit, and others. Each has a problem. Scrooge's problem, which he doesn't realize that he has, is that he lacks the Christmas Spirit. The Big Event is the appearance of Marley's Ghost.

During the middle of the story, three more spirits appear to Scrooge, but the Crisis comes when Scrooge sees his name on the tombstone. He asks the crisis question: Is this fate or can I change? The story ends with Scrooge getting the Christmas Spirit and helping the others solve their problems.

Note that we are allowed to catch our breath after each apparition. In other words, this story is well paced. Excitement and action are followed by reflection and reaction, and each turning point creates even more anticipation for the next, so that the story's high points get higher and higher until the end. In terms of dramatic tension and conflict, your story also needs peaks and valleys. Remember that the peaks should get generally higher as the story progresses.

Of Mints and Men
I'll take a moment here and offer a letter from a student who thanked me for bringing mints to class and demonstrated her clear understanding of basic story structure. She writes:

"It was ironic that I met another writer who shared my addiction to starlight mints. In my case, it began as an innocent habit. I would keep a jar of mints beside my computer so I could have a little pick-me-up at any time during the day. THE SET UP. Then a trip to the dentist revealed I had my first cavity in twelve years. BIG EVENT. Things went from bad to worse as I missed dentist appointments, spent the housekeeping money on starlight mints, and couldn't even kiss my husband because of all the mints crammed into my mouth. PLOT COMPLICATIONS. Until the CRISIS MOMENT, when my husband told me that I had to choose between starlight mints or our marriage. I made the agonizing decision to give up mints. I'm happy now and my marriage is stronger than ever. RESOLUTION."

Does the movie AIRPLANE use story structure? Yes. Any comedy that tells a story has a story structure. AIRPLANE is the story of a man who has lost his nerve to fly and who must regain it to save the people on the airplane. Here's a quote from the writers of AIRPLANE and NAKED GUN, Zucker, Abrahams, and Zucker. (This appeared in *The Hollywood Scriptwriter.*)

"The movies appear to be a kind of screen anarchy, but believe me, the process of getting it up there is much different. I mean, we're not maniacs, we don't bounce off the walls when we write. It gets to be a very scientifically designed process, actually. We spend a lot of time . . . marking off the three acts, concentrating not on the jokes but on the structure and sequence of the story. It's a very dull first couple of months, but that's how we spend them."

Situation, conflict, and resolution—the flow of the story

MAKE A GOOD FIRST IMPRESSION

The first thing your script should be concerned with is hooking the reader and setting forth the rules of that story. If the opening scene has bombs and car crashes in it, it is called the hook. Otherwise, it's called the opening scene, but you still want it to hook the reader of your script.

Obviously, the opening image—the first thing we see—makes your first impression. It implies something about your story—the location, the mood, a symbol, or even the theme.

BODY HEAT opens with "Flames in the night sky."

APOCALYPSE NOW opens with a jungle aflame and the surreal sounds of helicopters. Superimposed over this is Martin Sheen watching a ceiling fan that reminds him of helicopter rotors. He is recalling his last mission. What this writer/director is doing is setting the standards by which we'll measure the rest of the story. He defines the context of his story. Just as a character should stay in character, so should your story stay in character.

What is the character of your story? It will include the atmosphere or mood, the location, the emotional setting, and the genre. Genre refers to the type of movie; for example, action/adventure, Western, thriller, romantic comedy, sci-fi, family drama, and so forth.

In GHOSTBUSTERS, we see a librarian scared by a ghost and laugh our heads off. Supernatural comedy. Then we see Bill Murray hitting on a coed. There's probably a thousand ways to portray this, but the writers stay in the genre. Bill Murray pretends the coed has ESP and that she needs his tutelage to understand her gift.

BLADERUNNER opens with a "guided tour" of a definite future place while setting the mood of the story.

In STAR WARS, the rules of the game, the nature of the weaponry, the limits of the technology, and the two conflicting sides are all introduced early.

My screenplay THE SECRET OF QUESTION MARK CAVE opens with children at play. I want to establish early on that we are to behold the world through the eyes of a child and believe in imagination.

YOUR TWO KEY CHARACTERS

Early in your script, you'll want to introduce us to your central character, sometimes called the *pivotal character*. Often this person will appear in the opening scene. Obviously, the primary opposition character must be introduced as well. This person does not have to appear as early, but could. Dramatic choice.

The protagonist is the good guy or hero, while the antagonist is the bad guy. Usually the protagonist is also the central character, but sometimes the role of central character goes to the antagonist. In AMADEUS, Salieri, the bad guy, is the main cause of action and, therefore, the central character around whom the story is built. His opponent is Mozart, the good guy.

In THE HAND THAT ROCKS THE CRADLE, Peyton, the nanny, is the central character because she has the goal that drives the story. Claire, the wife, is the primary opposition character even though she is the protagonist. Marlene is a secondary opposition character.

One key to making a drama dramatic is to create a strong central character with a powerful goal, and then provide a strong opposition character who tries to stop the central character from achieving the goal. This assures us of conflict. And conflict is drama.

THE CATALYST

You've heard the horror stories of readers, agents, and executives reading the first few pages of a script and then tossing it on the dung heap. One way to avoid that is for something to happen early on. I recall how delighted my agent was when he told me about a script he had just read, REGARDING HENRY. "He's shot on page seven! Imagine, shot on page seven!" He emphasized "page seven" for my benefit because I was late getting things moving in the script he was representing at that time.

Somewhere in the first ten or fifteen pages of your script, something should happen to give the central character a goal, desire, mission, need, or problem. I like to call this event the *Catalyst*, or *Inciting Incident*. Yes, it is a turning point. No, it's not usually the same as the Big Event, although it could be. This term and many other terms are used in a variety of ways by industry people. One person's Catalyst is another person's First Major Turning Point. The key is to understand the *principle*.

Here's the principle: When a story begins, life is in balance. Yes, your hero may have a problem, but it's a problem he's always had. Luke Skywalker, in STAR WARS, wants to become a pilot, but he's stuck on the farm. It's a problem he's always had. Life is in balance.

Then the Catalyst kicks things out of balance and gives the central character a new problem, need, goal, desire. The rest of the movie is spent getting things back into balance. For Luke Skywalker, the Catalyst is when he tinkers with R2-D2 and accidentally triggers a holographic image of Princess Leia saying, "Help me Obi-wan, you're my only hope." Now Luke has a desire to help Princess Leia and find Obi-wan Kenobi (Old Ben). Luke's life will not find a new equilibrium until the Death Star is destroyed. The Big Event is Luke's return home to find his aunt and uncle have been slaughtered. Now he joins with Obi-wan to fight the empire.

In WITNESS, an Amish boy witnesses a murder. It feels like the Big Event, but it can't be because it doesn't happen to the central character, Harrison Ford. It's the Catalyst. It creates a problem or desire for Harrison Ford. Now he wants to solve the murder. Now the movie's moving. In other words, the Catalyst begins the movement of the story. But the Big Event in WITNESS occurs at the police office.

The little boy peers through the trophy case and spots a picture of the killer. Harrison Ford realizes that the murderer is on the police force. He goes to the chief and reports. The chief asks, "Have you told anyone else?" Harrison Ford says, "I haven't told anyone." Then when he goes home, he's shot. He knows they'll attempt to kill the boy next, so he rushes to the boy and his mother and together they escape to Act 2 and the world of the Amish.

Do you see that the Big Event is bigger than the Catalyst? In CHINATOWN, the first Mrs. Mulwray who hires Jake is the Catalyst. She gives Jake a mission. But the Big Event is when the real Mrs. Mulwray shows up.

In PRETTY WOMAN, Richard Gere and Julia Roberts meet. Catalyst. He pays her to stay with him at the hotel. Big Event.

THELMA AND LOUISE: They leave town to go fishing. Catalyst. Louise shoots Thelma's attacker. Big Event.

You may ask: Can the Catalyst also be the Big Event? Sure. GHOST and REGARD-ING HENRY are two examples. Keep in mind that I am presenting guidelines in this book, not hard-and-fast rules.

A good catalyst, besides giving the central character a new problem or desire, will often reveal something of the main conflict, story premise, or situation. For example, will Harrison Ford (in WITNESS) catch the killer? Will E.T. get home? Will Roy Scheider get Jaws? Will Richard Gere and Julia Roberts find true love in PRETTY WOMAN? Can Diane Keaton have it all—a family and a career—in BABY BOOM?

FORESHADOWING

Since Act 1 is primarily devoted to setting up the story situation, foreshadowing becomes a vital tool. In the first act of ALIENS, we establish early on that Sigourney Weaver can operate a combination loader/fork lift. This large contraption works on hydraulics and is literally an extension of her arms and legs. That's the set-up. At the end of the movie, she uses it to fight the big mama alien. That's the payoff.

In many James Bond movies, Q gives James his gadgets. They can be pretty ridiculous, but as long as they are established early, we believe them. However, if at the end of the movie James saved himself with a tiny midget missile that carried a 100-megaton nuclear warhead, we'd say, "Where did that come from?" And we'd feel ripped off—right?

Here's the point: You can get away with almost anything if you will set it up, or foreshadow it, early in your story. Much of screenwriting is setting things up for a later payoff.

HIGH NOON is a wonderful example of foreshadowing. The audience is made aware of the terrible thing that might happen at high noon. This foreshadowing helps motivate conflicts between Gary Cooper and his wife, and with certain members of the town.

In an early scene of GHOST, Patrick Swayze watches an airline disaster on the news and comments at how quickly life can end. Later he confides in Demi Moore that he is afraid—every time something good happens in his life, something bad happens. There is a foreshadowing here of his imminent death. There is also a suspenseful moment where a statue of an angel is moved into the apartment. Can you guess what this foreshadows?

A word of caution on the first act taken as a whole: Don't provide too much information or exposition. Only give the audience what they need to understand the story without getting confused.

THE PINCH AND RISING CONFLICT

The beginning ends with the Big Event. The middle focuses primarily on the conflict and complications of the story. The central character emerges from Act 1 with a desire to do something about the difficult situation created by the Big Event. Her action will likely fail, forcing her to take new actions. There will be many setbacks in Act 2 and some breakthroughs or temporary triumphs.

Remember, the long middle section (Act 2) focuses on a *rising* conflict. Your reader will lose interest in a conflict that merely repeats. Strong subplots that crisscross with the main plot will help you avoid repetitive conflict.

At the *Pinch* of the story, around page 60, another major event occurs. The central character often becomes fully committed. This is when Scarlet O'Hara makes her famous vow before intermission: "I'll never go hungry again." The Pinch can also be the moment when the motivation to achieve the goal becomes fully clear, or the stakes are raised. In GHOST, this is when Patrick Swayze, as a ghost, learns that his best friend is the one who had him killed.

In DAVE, the Pinch is when Dave defies the press secretary and acts as president. This is truly a Point of No Return for Dave, the point when he becomes fully committed.

From the Pinch on, the central character takes even stronger actions, perhaps even desperate actions that threaten to compromise her values. One or more temporary triumphs arouse the opposition, who now shows his true strength. There may be a major setback, followed often by a new revelation or inspiration.

This is when Tom Cruise discovers that Dustin Hoffman, Raymond, is the Rain Man of his childhood, and that his dad protected Tom as a baby by putting the Rain Man (Raymond) in an institution.

The conflict intensifies, the pace quickens until the worst thing that could happen happens. This is the Crisis, the point when all seems lost, or where the character faces a crucial decision. The worst thing that could happen to Indiana Jones is to be locked in a tomb with thousands of snakes while his enemies get away with the world's most important artifact.

THE RESOLUTION

As you know, the Climax or Showdown follows on the heels of the Crisis. Often, someone or something spurs the character on to the Showdown. The goal—everything—is on the line, including the theme or movie message (discussed later) and/or some important value.

There's something you should know about the final act. It's not mandatory to have car chases and car crashes in it. In MOONSTRUCK, everyone simply gathers around the breakfast table. It's the big scene at the end—the biggest scene in the movie, where everything comes together. It's the Showdown. The Showdown is bigger than the Big Event. It's the biggest event (or series of events) in the movie because everything, up until now, has led up to it.

During this climactic scene or sequence (or just afterward), the central character realizes something new about herself, or we see some visible or spoken evidence of her growth. The central character has been through a crucible, has shown great courage—physical, emotional, and/or moral courage—and now the final result must be revealed to the audience and understood by the central character. We'll discuss this *Realization* later.

Finally, we have the *Denouement*, where all the loose ends are tied together and any remaining subplots are resolved. In BACK TO THE FUTURE, we see how Marty's family turn out, and the professor returns from the future with a stunning new outfit.

Now please don't internalize this as a formula. Genres vary. Forms vary. There are many ways to tell a story. Your basic structure may change or evolve as you write; and keep in mind that every story has its own structure, its own life, its own way of unfolding.

Note: For a summary review of the function of each of these key turning points, see pages 116-118.

The low down on high concept

A TITILLATING TITLE

Every screenplay and teleplay needs a titillating title. Of course, from the very beginning you'll want a working title to inspire you. The title you choose for your completed work should be short enough to fit on the marquee. Ideally, it conveys something about the concept or theme. Like the heading in an ad, the title must stop the reader and pull him into the story. For example, the title STAR WARS instantly conveys something of the story.

BODY HEAT and IN COLD BLOOD throw light on the subject matter and genre. DIE HARD and DIRTY DANCING are both million-dollar titles.

KINDERGARTEN COP communicates the concept: Hard-boiled cop becomes kindergarten teacher. That concept pops out and instantly tells you, "I'm a movie."

Although a little long, HONEY, I SHRUNK THE KIDS is a superb title. It instantly conveys a feeling for the story.

An example of an ineffective title might be RAIDERS OF THE LOST ARK. I heard Sydney Ganis explain how much he worried about this title. (Mr. Ganis was the marketer of this project.) Is this the football Raiders? Is this Noah's ark? How is this title going to fit on the marquee? Not to worry. The movie had good word of mouth and a heck of an advertising budget, so it didn't matter.

However, an effective and titillating title can make an important first impression for your script, especially if it hints of a high concept.

IT'S GOTTA BE BIG

A lot has been said about *high concept*. Producers will tell you that most spec scripts that are bought are bought on the concept. The higher the concept, the easier the sale. So what is high concept? I've gleaned answers to this question from a variety of sources.

- Easily understood by an eighth grader
- Can be encapsulated in a sentence or two
- Provocative and big—you know immediately it's a hit
- Character plus conflict plus a hook (the hook is often the Big Event)
- It has legs—it can stand on its own without stars
- A fresh and highly marketable idea
- Unique with familiar elements

Here's Jeffrey Katzenberg as quoted in *Variety*: "In the dizzying world of movie making, we must not be distracted from one fundamental concept: The idea is king. If a movie begins with a great, original idea, chances are good it will be successful, even if it is executed only marginally well."

What if babies could talk? That's a hot concept. Tell me more. *What if a baby, who had a mommy but not a daddy, could talk? . . . And this baby wants John Travolta for a daddy, but mommy hates him.* Does this sound like a pitch for LOOK WHO'S TALKING?

A teenage computer hacker breaks into the Pentagon computer system. In the end, he prevents World War III. WAR GAMES.

The concept is important for another reason. It's what you lead with when you pitch your script. We'll cover the topic "How to Pitch Without Striking Out" in Book IV. What's important to realize now is this: The concept is what hooks—or fails to hook—the agent or producer.

When Gene Roddenberry pitched STAR TREK, he had problems. No one was interested in sci-fi. A popular TV show at the time was WAGON TRAIN. So Gene pitched STAR TREK like this: *WAGON TRAIN in space.* He hitched his "Star" to a "Wagon," and the rest is history. He combined the familiar with the unique.

ALIEN was pitched as *JAWS in space.* PASSENGER 57 is *DIE HARD on a plane.*

Here's your pitch for TOOTSIE: *A male-chauvinist actor masquerades as a woman to get a role in a soap opera.* As you can see, high concept does not necessarily mean action or high adventure. TOOTSIE is neither, but the concept is hot. It communicates much of the conflict and action of the story.

A radio talk-show host is out to redeem himself after his comments trigger a murderous act of a psychopath—FISHER KING.

What if Peter Pan grew up? Although not a complete story, it certainly sounds intriguing. Send me the script.

A word of caution
Don't worry about trends, and don't try to predict the market. Don't be overly concerned with what you think sells. Keep in mind that the "lower" the concept, the better the writing must be. Realize that most well-written spec scripts are not bought, but become writing samples that demonstrate the state of your craft. That spec script doesn't necessarily have to be high concept to entice a producer to offer you a writing assignment. For that reason, your first script should flow from your passion. Write about what *you* want to write about, while keeping the above in mind.

ADAPTATIONS

Don't adapt it until you own it. This is one of my few carved-in-stone rules. Don't adapt a novel or play unless you control the rights to the property. We'll discuss the acquisition of rights to true stories, books, and plays in Book IV. There are basically three steps to writing an adaptation.

1. Read the novel or play for an understanding of the essential story, the relationships, the goal, the need, the primary conflict, and the subtext.

2. Identify the five to ten best scenes. These are the basis for your script.

3. Write an original script.

A script cannot hope to cover all the internal conflict that the novel does, nor can it include all the subplots that a long novel can. This is why novel lovers often hate movie versions.

Jurassic Park is a novel that was adapted to the screen. The book's central character is the billionaire, with the mathematician as the opposition character. The book is science-driven, an intellectual experience as much as an emotional experience. Spielberg saw the high concept: What if you could make dinosaurs from old DNA?

It's interesting to note the changes that transformed this book into a movie. First, the central character becomes the paleontologist. This provided a more youthful hero. Our paleontologist is given a flaw he didn't have in the book—he doesn't like children. He grows to like them by striving for his goal. Although there is no love interest in the book, Laura Dern fills that role in the movie. Although the character development in the movie is thin, these changes make for a more visual and emotionally accessible film. The focus of the movie, of course, is on the dinosaurs, the T-Rex in particular. Hey, movies are visual.

My favorite scene in the book—the moment at the end when the paleontologist realizes that the velociraptors want to migrate—is simply not visual enough for the movie; plus it doesn't have a strong bearing on the main action plot. I think the right choices were made.

Story layering, plot, and genre

Now that we have a basic understanding of how a story works, let's expand on that and deepen the story.

GOALS AND NEEDS

In every story, the central character has a conscious goal. The goal is whatever your central character outwardly strives for. Of course, opposition makes it *almost* impossible to reach the goal. That opposition usually comes in the form of a person who either wants the same goal or who, in some other way, directly opposes your central character's goal.

Beneath it all looms a great unconscious *need*. The need has to do with self-image, or finding love, or living a better life—whatever the character *needs* to be truly happy or fulfilled. This inner drive sometimes runs counter to the goal and sometimes supports or motivates it. The Crisis often brings the need into full consciousness.

Usually the need is blocked from within by a character flaw. This flaw serves as the inner opposition to the inner need. This character flaw is obvious to the audience, because we see the character hurting people, including himself. The flaw is almost always a form of selfishness, pride, or greed.

Where does the flaw come from? Usually the backstory. Something happened before the movie began that deeply hurt the character. Now he or she acts in inappropriate or hurtful ways. Let's see what we can learn about goals and needs from TWINS.

Danny DeVito is the Central Character. His conscious, measurable goal is $5 million. There is a strong outward opposition to this goal—a really bad guy wants the money as well.

DeVito also has a need that he himself is unaware of. He needs the love of a family. Blocking him is his own greed and selfishness—he's out for himself. This is the character flaw, and it is motivated by his backstory. His mother abandoned him, and he learned early that all people are out to get him, so he better get them first. DeVito can never have what he truly needs until he gives up his selfish point of view.

This is a neat little story because the goal and the need happen to be in opposition to each other at the Crisis. DeVito must choose between the two. He can escape with the money (his goal), but someone holds a gun on his brother (his need). What will Danny DeVito decide?

At this crisis moment, he finds himself unable to leave his brother. Why? In a later scene, we learn that he really cared and didn't fully realize it until the Crisis. That's why he turned around and willingly gave up the money to save his brother's life. Danny DeVito reformed. He gave up something he wanted for his brother. Fortunately, in the end, he gets both a family and the money. The writer gives the audience what they want, but not in the way they expect it. Don't you love those Hollywood endings?

TWO STORIES IN ONE

Screenplays often tell two main stories. The *Outside/Action Story* is driven by the goal. It is sometimes referred to as the *spine*.

The *Inside/Emotional Story* usually derives from a relationship and is generally driven by the need. It is sometimes referred to as the *heart of the story* or the *emotional through-line*. To find the Inside/Emotional Story, look in the direction of the key relationship in the story. Sometimes there is no inside story, no flaw, no need, as in many thrillers, action/adventures, and horror movies.

Each story—the Outside/Action Story and the Inside/Emotional Story—has its own turning points and structure. One is the main plot; the other, a subplot. Hopefully, the two stories are intertwined synergistically.

Again, TWINS serves as a good example. The Outside/Action story is driven by the $5 million goal, and the Inside/Emotional Story is driven by his need for a family. The action is what keeps us interested, but the emotion is what touches us. Although there are exceptions, the Inside/Emotional Story is what the movie is really about. The movie is really about a relationship.

In GONE WITH THE WIND, Scarlet has several goals. She wants to be seen by all the boys. She wants to get married. She wants never to eat radishes again. She wants to save Tara. And she wants Ashley, which is probably her main goal. Rather complex. It may even sound confusing until you realize the story is really about what she needs—Rhett Butler. Scarlet is outwardly striving for all the things just named, but she is not after Rhett. Nevertheless, the movie belongs to Scarlet and Rhett.

In ROMANCING THE STONE, what is Kathleen Turner outwardly striving for? She wants to find the stone so she can save her sister. Is this a clear and visual goal? Yes. Is she consciously aware that this is what she's after? Yes. Is her goal opposed by anyone? Yes. Zolo wants it, as do the kidnappers. And Michael Douglas wants the stone so he can buy a boat and sail around the world.

What does Kathleen Turner need? Romance. Is she striving for romance? No. She writes out her fantasies in her romance novels. Her flaw is simple indifference—she won't try. In this story, she gets what she needs by striving for the goal.

In my script-analysis work, I receive many scripts that are completely missing a goal. To illustrate, let's pretend I was a consultant for Diane Thomas when she first started writing. She tells me she has a script about a woman who goes on vacation to South America and falls in love with an adventurer. Sounds interesting, but it's not compelling enough. So I ask Diane about the goal.

"Happiness is her goal," she responds.

"Happiness is not a goal. It's too vague."

"Well . . . romance is her goal. That's it."

"That feels more like a need than a goal. It's actually part of your Inside/Emotional Story. You need an action track for this inside story to roll on."

"Well, vacationing is her goal. She consciously wants to have a good vacation. She deserves it after all that writing."

Diane relaxes. It appears as though she has a complete story now, but I disappoint her. "Technically, vacationing is a goal," I say, "but it does not stir my heart nor does it set up strong opportunities for conflict. Something has to *happen.*"

"I know!" Diane states triumphantly. "What if her sister is kidnapped and she has to save her?" Now Diane has a strong Big Event and a story.

This problem is so common that I strongly urge you to stop and examine your story. Are you missing an action track for your wonderful inside story to roll on?

Variations on the action and emotion tracks
In BACK TO THE FUTURE, the outside story plot, as you would expect, is action-oriented. It is driven by Marty's goal to get back to the future. So far so good. The inside story plot, however, is driven not by a need, but by a second goal: Marty wants to get his mom and dad back together again.

This results in twin crises at the end of the story, side by side. First, can Marty get his parents to kiss before he disappears into oblivion? This is the Inside/Emotional Story built around a relationship. Once resolved, Marty races from the dance to the Outside/Action Story: Can Marty, in the DeLorean, hit the wire at the same moment that lightning strikes the tower?

Is there an inner need in this movie? Yes, Marty needs a better family, and that's just what he gets in the end.

MOONSTRUCK. Cher's goal is to marry by the book. This goal is represented by Danny. She was married once before and it was unlucky because they didn't do it right, so "this time, Danny, you've got to have a ring and get on your knees and propose, and we're going to a priest because I'm doing this marriage by the book."

Cher *needs* to marry for love. This need is represented by Ronnie. This is not fully in her consciousness until she goes to the opera. Blocking her need is her character flaw—she's going to marry someone she doesn't love. This character flaw is motivated by her backstory of having an unlucky marriage. At the breakfast-table scene in the end, she admits that the need is more important to her than the goal.

HOME ALONE's Kevin strives to protect the house and himself from the Wet Bandits. That's the main action plot. The emotional story? He needs his family's acceptance, his mother's in particular. Two flaws block him. One, he's a brat; two, he is incompetent—he can't even tie his shoelaces. These are subplots. The first flaw hooks the parents in the audience—he becomes a son who learns to appreciate his mother and family. The second flaw hooks the kids—he becomes competent fighting the adult bandits. This is a coming-of-age subplot.

The mother's goal is to get home. Her need and flaw are similar to her son's. In fact, they are mirrors of each other. Another subplot involves the man with the shovel who wants to become reconciled to his son. It's not hard to see that the underlying theme of this flick is family reconciliation.

KRAMER VS. KRAMER: The goal? Custody. The need? To be a loving father. In this screenplay, the goal and the need oppose each other, creating a crisis. Dustin Hoffman loses custody in a court battle and wants to appeal. His attorney tells him: "It'll cost $15,000." No problem. Hoffman wants to go ahead. "You'll have to put Billy on the stand." Well, to put Billy on the stand could deeply hurt him. Hoffman loves him too much. He chooses to give up custody rather than hurt the child. He overcomes his selfishness and abandons his goal for custody.

There's another way to look at this. Think of yourself as the next great screenwriter creating this story from scratch. You know the story is going to be about Hoffman becoming a father, learning to love his son. So you, the writer, give Hoffman goals, behaviors, and desires that are flawed. You give him a main goal of gaining custody because you know it will eventually contrast with what he really needs, to unselfishly love his son. So Hoffman's goal in this story is flawed—it's not the best way to love his son or satisfy his inner drive to be a father. In the end, he becomes a father by giving up custody, by giving up the goal. In other words, he changes his method and grows into full fatherhood.

In THE WIZARD OF OZ, the main goal is Kansas; the need is to realize there's no place like home.

In SILENCE OF THE LAMBS, Clarice's goal is to save the woman from Buffalo Bill. Her need is to silence the lambs of her past. In this case, she fills her need by achieving her goal.

PRETTY WOMAN: Here we have two people who need love, but who are prostituting themselves. Their behavior does not harmonize with their need. In the end, they give up their old ways and thus fill their need. They grow.

My favorite romantic comedy is SOME LIKE IT HOT. Tony Curtis, posing as a millionaire, uses Marilyn Monroe. He *needs* to love her. Marilyn Monroe's goal is to marry a millionaire. She chases after Tony Curtis because she thinks he is one. Her unconscious need, however, is to marry for love. The Crisis comes when Tony Curtis is forced by Spats Columbo, a gangster, to leave Marilyn. At that point, Tony realizes he is actually in love with Marilyn. He realizes what a jerk he is and vows to get out of her life. He'll do what's best for her and leave without her. Marilyn, however, realizes that he's the one, even though he's not really a millionaire. She chases after him. Together for the right reasons, they sail off into the sunset.

In love stories, one or both characters is willing to give up something in the end for the other. That something is often a goal related to their flaw. In PRETTY WOMAN, Richard Gere not only gives up his questionable business practices, but he also overcomes his fear of heights. Love stories are essentially about two people transforming each other and learning to love each other. PRETTY WOMAN is pretty good at doing just that.

PLOT

Up until now, we've explained the outside/action plot and the inside/emotional plot. I'm using the word "plot" as a noun here. The verb *to plot* is a creative process that uses character and story structure. When all the plotting is over, you end up with a *plot* and several *subplots*.

Plot comprises the important events in a character's story. The words *plot, structure,* and *story* are often used interchangeably. Plot grows from character because everything starts with a character who has a goal. Since the goal is opposed, the character takes action. The resulting conflict culminates in a crisis. Will she win? Will he lose? Will he grow? Will she decline? The answer to those questions determines the kind of story—the kind of plot—you're writing.

There are basically two kinds of stories: plot-driven stories (which I prefer to call goal-driven stories) and character-driven stories. In goal-driven stories, the focus is primarily on the character's goal and the action—the spine of the story. In character-driven stories, the focus is primarily on character dynamics and a key relationship—the heart of the story. First, let's look at some examples of goal-driven stories.

• **The character wins.** In this plot model, the character strives for a goal and wins. Very simple and very common. Examples include: ROCKY, DIE HARD, THE FUGITIVE, SILENCE OF THE LAMBS, A FEW GOOD MEN, UNDER SIEGE, RUDY, TRUE LIES, SPEED, and THE KARATE KID.

• **The character loses.** With this plot, a moral victory of some kind often results despite the failure of a very sympathetic character. SPARTACUS fails to achieve his goal for the slaves and is crucified, but sees his wife and child escape to freedom. THELMA & LOUISE never get to Mexico, but in the attempt they achieve a certain freedom. Other examples are ONE FLEW OVER THE CUCKOO'S NEST, FROM HERE TO ETERNITY, THE MISSION (here, they flat-out lose), and JFK (the Jim Garrison character).

• **The character sows the seeds of his own destruction.** What Goes Around, Comes Around. Examples include: FRANKENSTEIN, DANGEROUS LIAISONS, ALL THE KING'S MEN, and MOBY DICK.

The following plot models seem more focused on character dynamics, and on the Inside/Emotional Story.

• **The character grows by doing the right thing.** Here, the character is about to do the wrong thing, but transforms into someone who overcomes his or her flaw, and does the right thing. Very popular in Hollywood. In CASABLANCA, Rick wants to get even with Ilsa; in the end, he does the right thing and helps her and her husband escape. Tom Cruise, in RAIN MAN, wants his inheritance; in the end, he tears up the check and does the right thing for his brother.

Other examples include: ON THE WATERFRONT, THE PRINCE AND THE PAUPER and its modern counterpart, TRADING PLACES, THE SCENT OF A WOMAN, THE DOCTOR, AN OFFICER AND A GENTLEMAN, and THE CRYING GAME.

Romantic comedies usually fit this plot model because one or more of the lovers give up something for the other. In PRETTY WOMAN, both characters give up their careers. In SOME LIKE IT HOT, the lovers stop using each other. MIDNIGHT RUN is a love story without the romance—both Robert DeNiro and Charles Grodin give up their goals for each other in the end.

• **The character grows up.** Here the character comes of age while striving for one or more goals that are either achieved or not achieved—it doesn't matter which. We don't really care whether the boys are first to find the body in STAND BY ME. What we care about is the relationship and growth of the boys. The goal is only there to give the relationship a track to roll on. In some character-driven stories, the goal may change. And that's fine as long as the conflict intensifies and rises to a crisis and showdown.

Here are more examples of characters growing up: RISKY BUSINESS, HOOK (Peter Pan grows up), BREAKING AWAY, PLATOON, AMERICAN GRAFFITI, SUMMER OF '42, and FALLING DOWN (the Robert Duvall character).

• **The character learns.** Here, the character learns what he or she needs to be happy. Jimmy Stewart realizes he has a wonderful life in IT'S A WONDERFUL LIFE. David Niven learns what's important in life in THE BISHOP'S WIFE. Harold, in HAROLD AND MAUDE, discovers that life is worth living. In THE WIZARD OF OZ, Dorothy finds out there's no place like home. She also achieves her goal of returning to Kansas. (An argument could be made that the main plot is a Character-Wins Plot and that the realization of her need is merely a subplot that supports the goal.) Other examples: THE PRINCE OF TIDES—Nick Nolte learns he wants to live with his family. In CITY SLICKERS, Billy Crystal finally figures out the meaning of life.

• **The character fails to learn.** Here, the character fails to learn what he or she needs to learn to be happy. In this plot, the character does not grow, but the audience learns the lesson. Examples include WAR OF THE ROSES, GOODFELLAS, and RAGING BULL. In BUTCH CASSIDY AND THE SUNDANCE KID, Paul Newman and Robert Redford never figure out that they are in the wrong line of work and need to change with the times.

• **The character declines,** often by striving to achieve a worthy goal. Here are your examples: LAWRENCE OF ARABIA, UNFORGIVEN, CITIZEN KANE, and FALLING DOWN (the Michael Douglas character). In the beginning of THE GODFATHER, Michael (the central character) is something of a patriot who doesn't want a part of the family business. In the end, he *runs* the family business, but his rise is also his decline, which is demonstrated in the final scene where he lies, straight-faced, to his wife.

These broad plot models are presented to help you understand how stories work. They are not all-inclusive. In virtually all stories, there is one main plot. Everything else happening in the character's life is a subplot. In addition to the central character's plot and subplot, each of the other characters in the screenplay has his or her own plot with a goal, action, crisis, and resolution. These are all subplots.

Furthermore, each character's crisis may come at a different juncture in the script, or may converge at the same crisis moment, depending on the story. The great secret to master-plotting is to bring the various subplots and main plot into conflict. In other words, most or all of the subplots should cross the central character's main purpose.

When two characters are at cross purposes, you have a *Unity of Opposites*. To insure a conflict to the end, you need a unity of the central character's main plot and the opposing character's plot. The unity exists when the two plots are in direct opposition to each other, and compromise is impossible, insuring a struggle to the end. For example, in FATAL ATTRACTION, a married man has an affair with a beautiful blonde and wants to terminate the relationship with her, but he can't because she carries his baby and is fixated on him. There exists a *Unity of Opposites*. He wants to end the relationship. She wants the relationship to grow. Compromise is impossible.

GENRE

Another element to consider in plotting is genre. This is because each genre carries with it certain characteristics. For example, in the love story, one or both lovers will change in some way. Most often, this results in a Character-Grows-by-Doing-the-Right-Thing Plot.

Action/adventure stories often open with an exciting action sequence, followed by some exposition. Although these can be suspenseful, the key to this genre is action. These stories follow a Character-Wins Plot and usually end with a chase and/or plenty of violence.

With the thriller, the focus is on suspense more than action. In a thriller, an ordinary man or woman gets involved in a situation that becomes life-threatening. The bad guys desperately want the *MacGuffin*, a name Hitchcock gave to the plot-device that often drives the thriller. In NORTH BY NORTHWEST, the MacGuffin is government secrets. In CHARADE, it's $250,000 in stamps. Although the characters are after the MacGuffin, the audience cares more about the survival of the central character. This is because he or she cannot get help, has been betrayed in some way, and cannot trust anyone. The primary motivation is one of survival, so there's not much of a Character Realization in the end.

The horror story differs from the thriller in that the opposition is a monster, or a monster-like human. This genre leans heavily on shock and surprise.

The murder mystery opens with a murder. Then, the police officer, private detective, or retired novelist solves the case. Since solving the case is primarily a mental exercise, there is often a voice-over narration so we can be privy to the central character's thoughts, as in MAGNUM, P.I. If this central character is a private detective, he will usually be portrayed as one who operates on the fringes of the law, such as Jake Gittes in CHINATOWN.

Obviously, there are many genres and combinations of genres: Western, Historical Epic, Romantic Comedy, Traveling Angel, Buddy Picture, Fish-out-of-Water-Fantasy-Action-Romance, and on and on. Once you choose your genre, watch several representative films. You are not researching your story but understanding what makes the genre work.

MYTH

Beyond genre and plot is myth. In any story you write, it may help you to understand the mythological journey. The "hero's journey," as presented by Joseph Campbell, follows a particular pattern that may be weaved into the fabric of any story, regardless of its genre. Many stories contain elements of this mythological journey, while a few, like STAR WARS, can be called myths because the central character passes through each stage of the hero's journey. Briefly, these are the stages in the hero's journey:

The hero lives amid ordinary surroundings. The Catalyst is actually a call to adventure, but the hero is reluctant to heed the call. This could be the moment when the hero receives her mission. She is given an amulet or aid of some kind by an older person, a mentor. For example, Dorothy is given the ruby red slippers by a good witch. Luke is given the light saber by Obi-Wan.

The central character travels to the extraordinary world. This is followed by a series of tests and obstacles. The hero often undergoes a death experience and enters the secret hideout, the witch's castle, the deathstar, the belly of the whale, or the innermost cave.

Finally, the hero seizes the treasure and is chased back to the ordinary world, where this treasure will bless the people. The grail heals the land. The hero may be resurrected in some way. Luke and Han are honored at an awards ceremony. Dorothy returns to her family. The LAST STARFIGHTER is transfigured in front of the townspeople. Oskar Schindler is resurrected in a ring ceremony.

As a writer, you may have heard a call to action, a call to write, but hesitated. You must heed the call. As you struggle, as you learn, and as you write, you may very well walk the path of the hero, overcome obstacles, gain allies, and become the next great screenwriter. The hero's journey may very well become your personal odyssey.

Note: This is a good time to do Steps 1, 2, and 3 in the workbook (Book III).

Ten keys to creating captivating characters

Your central character requires ten things from a writer. Keep in mind as we review these that virtually all of them apply to supporting characters, and even minor characters, as well as to your main characters.

A GOAL AND AN OPPOSITION

Your character wants a goal. A dramatic goal is specific and measurable. Dealing with life is not a goal. Happiness is not a goal. Seeking $10 million worth of doubloons on an old Spanish shipwreck off the Florida Keys is a goal. Winning the Pan American Ballroom Dance Competition is a goal. Getting the broomstick of the wicked witch in order to return to Kansas is a goal. The nature of the goal reveals a lot about your character.

Whatever the goal is, it should not be easy to attain. There must be opposition to the goal. Opposition creates conflict, and conflict makes drama. The opposition should be an individual. If it is an organization, let someone represent that organization. In GHOSTBUSTERS, the Environmental Protection Agency is represented by a man who makes it his personal business to bust the Ghostbusters.

In situations where a group opposes the central character, such as a gang, focus on one person in that group who stands as the greatest personal threat to the central character. Personalizing the opposition will create greater drama and will elicit the audience's sympathy for the central character. The hero is often defined by his/her opposition.

It is possible to have a nonhuman opposition, such as the forces of Nature, or even a monster (such as the Great White in JAWS). If you do have such an opposition, consider adding a human opponent as well. In JAWS, the mayor of Amity serves as a secondary opponent to Roy Scheider. In ALIENS, Burke is a strong secondary opponent. In fact, a well-written story often features three opponents.

In addition to the goal, you may wish to give your character some related inner drive or yearning that either supports the goal or is in opposition to the goal. This inner need may be inwardly blocked by some character flaw. This was discussed more fully in the preceding section.

MOTIVATION

Your character must be motivated. Ask yourself this question: *Why* does my character want what he wants? The answer to that question is the motivation. And the more personal, the better. In fact, the more personal it is, the more the audience will identify and sympathize with the character. It's the emotional touchstone between your audience and your character.

What is Rocky's goal in the first ROCKY movie? His goal is very specific. He wants to go the distance with the champ—fifteen rounds. Why? *To prove he's not a bum.* It's the personal motivation that gives the story its power. Personally, I hate boxing. I could care less who won the Thrilla in Manilla. And yet I've watched four of the Rocky movies. Why? Well, it's not for the boxing scenes. It's for the motivation behind those boxing scenes.

In the second ROCKY movie, his wife goes into a coma. Then she blinks her eyes open and says, "Win." Now Rocky has a motive for winning.

In ROCKY III, Mr. T has a tiff with Rocky's manager, Burgess Meredith. Meredith suffers a heart attack and dies. Does Rocky want to clean Mr. T's plow? Absolutely, and so does everyone in the theater.

In RAIN MAN, Tom Cruise's perception of his father's past harsh treatment of him motivates his goal of collecting the inheritance. In other words, he wants the inheritance to get even with his father.

JAWS is a horror movie complete with body parts and a monster. The only personal motivation needed here is survival, but the writer adds something very personal. When Brody fails to close the beach, a boy is eaten by JAWS. At the funeral, the mother slaps Brody's face in front of the entire town and says, "You killed my son." Now Brody wants not only to protect the town, but redeem himself.

The motivation often grows with the conflict. It becomes stronger as the story progresses. In AMADEUS, Salieri has many reasons for disliking Mozart. It seems that whenever they are together, Mozart finds a way to insult Salieri, even if it's innocently done. These accumulate over time. The clincher, however, is when Mrs. Mozart visits Salieri. She brings her husband's work with her and confesses that they need money and wonders if Salieri will help them. Salieri scrutinizes the manuscripts, and sees that these are first and only drafts of music, and notices no corrections. From Salieri's point of view, Mozart must simply be taking dictation from God. Salieri takes it personally. He goes to his private room and throws his crucifix into the fire. "From now on we are enemies," he says. Why?

Because God chose a degenerate like Mozart over him, Salieri, whose only wish has been to serve God through music. So here we have the goal—to fight God by killing Mozart—and the motivation—because God is unjust.

A BACKSTORY

Before page one of your screenplay, something significant happens to your central character. That event is called the *backstory*.

In ORDINARY PEOPLE, the backstory involves two brothers, teenagers, boating on a lake. A storm capsizes the boat and one drowns. The other blames himself and tries to kill himself. The script begins when he returns from the hospital.

IN SLEEPLESS IN SEATTLE, the backstory is the death of Tom Hanks' wife.

In the above examples, we are given quick glimpses of the backstory. Most often, the backstory is not seen by the audience, but it is there, haunting the central character and affecting her actions.

In THELMA & LOUISE, Louise was raped in Texas. It's what makes it possible for her to shoot Thelma's attacker. This backstory is not revealed to Thelma or the audience until much later in the story.

In UNFORGIVEN, Clint Eastwood was a killer before his wife reformed him.

In STARMAN, the backstory is the death of Karen Allen's husband.

The backstory can be subtle. For example, in FOUL PLAY, Goldie Hawn was once in love and it ended badly. It's as simple as that. At the beginning of the movie, we see a cautious Goldie Hawn, a person not quite ready for a new lover, particularly if it's Chevy Chase. It's easy to see how the backstory gives rise to the flaw that blocks the need. In the case of Goldie Hawn, she needs to feel safe with a man. She's not approachable because she's afraid.

In ORDINARY PEOPLE, Timothy Hutton's need is to forgive himself for his brother's accidental death. His flaw is that he tries to control his feelings too much and is self-accusing. This all emerges from his backstory.

In STARMAN, Karen Allen's need is to learn to live again now that her husband is dead.

In the CHINATOWN love scene, Mrs. Mulwray asks Jake why he avoids Chinatown. He explains, "I thought I was keeping someone from being hurt and actually I ended up making sure she was hurt." Jake is referring to his backstory, a traumatic event that transpired before the movie began. In the climactic showdown, Jake tries to keep Mrs. Mulwray from getting hurt and, in so doing, inadvertently facilitates her death. The backstory foreshadows the resolution.

SILENCE OF THE LAMBS: When Jodie Foster was a little girl, her dad, a police officer, was killed. She went to live on a ranch. One night they were slaughtering lambs and they were crying. She picked up a lamb and ran, but she wasn't strong enough. They caught up with her and slaughtered the lamb. Her need became to silence those cries. When a woman is captured by Buffalo Bill and placed in a pit, that woman becomes a crying lamb that Jodie Foster wants to save. But is she strong enough? She is. After she saves the woman, she gets a call from Dr. Lector. "Well, Clarice, have you silenced the lambs." That's the *Realization*. We know she has.

Occasionally, the audience is actually shown the backstory. In FLATLINERS, we see each main character's backstory at the appropriate moment in the script. THE PHILADELPHIA STORY, BACKDRAFT, and VERTIGO open with a backstory.

In CASABLANCA, the backstory is revealed in a flashback. In NUTS, Richard Dreyfuss must unravel Barbara Streisand's backstory to win the case.

THE WILL TO ACT

How do you judge a person? By words? Or by actions? Don't actions weigh more heavily than words for you? As the saying goes, "What you do sounds so loud in my ears, I cannot hear what you say."

Action reveals character, and crisis reveals his true colors, because a person does what he does because of who he is. Problems and obstacles reveal what he's made of. Since actions speak louder than words, your character will reveal more through action than through dialogue. Yes, dialogue can tell us a lot, particularly about what is going on inside, but actions tell us more.

Running Bear is a Sioux hunting buffalo on the wide prairie. This is interesting action. The buffalo are the opposition. But how can we make this more dramatic? Suppose the white settler's son is in the buffalo's path. The white man is Running Bear's enemy. But now Running Bear must make a decision that will reveal his true character. He decides to save the boy. Now he has an action—to save the boy from the herd.

Okay, let's take this one step further. The boy's father looks through the window and sees his son, and the buffalo; then to his horror, he sees his enemy, Running Bear. He thinks Running Bear is trying to kill his son. He grabs his rifle and races outside. Now we really care about the outcome. This is drama—characters in willful conflict.

A POINT OF VIEW AND ATTITUDES

Everyone has a belief system, a perception of reality that is influenced by past experience, a point of view that has developed over time. Our current experience is filtered through our past experience. This means two people may react in totally different ways to the same stimulus. It depends on their perception. Their point of view is expressed in attitudes.

Some time ago, I was in a department store. I found a little three-year-old who was alone and crying. I tried to calm her down so I could find her mother. The problem was her mother found me, and guess what she thought I was. That's right, Chester the Molester. Her perception was understandable, given the times we live in; but it was not reality. We don't see reality the way it is, we see it through the filter of our past experience.

Your character also has a past. We're going to discuss how to create that past shortly, but for right now realize that your character has a point of view expressed through attitudes. What is your character's point of view about life? What is your character's concept of love? How does he or she view the opposite sex? What is your character's attitude toward growing old? sex? falling rain? grocery shopping? dental hygiene and regular professional care? Is happiness a warm puppy or a warm gun?

Sol Stein recommends that you "give each character a separate set of facts. Don't give them the same view of the story." Your character will act from his or her point of view or belief system, regardless of how that point of view squares with reality. Salieri believes that great music comes from God. Therefore, Mozart must be God's creature on Earth.

In STARMAN, an alien creature crash-lands in Wisconsin. He is a being of light who floats over to Karen Allen's house. Karen has withdrawn from life because her husband was killed. The alien finds a lock of her husband's hair and clones himself a body. Now he looks just like her husband. He then makes her drive him to Arizona, which is where his mothership will pick him up. The alien's motivation for this goal is to get home. (This is "E.T. meets IT HAPPENED ONE NIGHT.") His point of view of life happens to be *life is precious*.

Karen Allen's goal is to escape. Her motivation is to be safe from the alien and also to be safe from her past. And the alien looks just like her past. The writer has taken her inside problem and put it on the outside to make it visual. Karen's point of view of life or belief is that life is scary: Husbands die (the backstory) and aliens kidnap you (the action story).

At the Pinch, Karen observes the alien as he brings a dead deer to life. This action emerges from his belief that life is precious. Touched by this action, her goal of escape is displaced by a desire to help Starman. This new goal is motivated by his inspiring action. Her point of view of life changes as well. Life is not so scary.

This story uses the deer as a metaphor. Karen Allen is the dead deer that Starman brings back to life (the emotional story). Her perception of life changes. And that's the key. When a character's point of view changes, that's character growth.

ROOM TO GROW

Your central character also has a point of view of herself. This point of view of self is called self-concept. *I'm a winner, I'm a loser. I'm clumsy, I'm graceful.* All of us act from this point of view of ourselves, and so do your characters. Here's what happens in the well-written story:

Metaphorically speaking, your character is a fish. The Big Event pulls him out of the water. He tries to swim. It's worked in the past, but it doesn't work now. And so he is forced to take new actions, different actions, but things get more and more difficult right up to the Crisis. Mustering all the courage and faith he has, he takes the last final action; then he emerges from the climax with a new self-concept—he's a fish no longer.

This moment is the *Realization*—the character realizes a change has taken place. Usually the Realization follows the Showdown (or climax), but it can take place during the Showdown or just before. It's a key emotional moment for your audience.

In GHOST, Patrick Swayze's growth is demonstrated at the end when he's finally able to say "I love you" to Demi Moore, instead of "ditto." Swayze also grows in another way—from mortal to guardian angel to heavenly being. Beginning, middle, end.

In A CHRISTMAS CAROL, Scrooge needs the Christmas Spirit. His attitude toward Christmas is neatly summed up in two words of dialogue: "Bah, humbug." The story is about transforming his belief. In the end, the change of character is revealed through his charitable actions and words.

Dustin Hoffman states his realization in TOOTSIE as follows: "I was a better man as a woman with you than I was as a man. I just have to do it without the dress."

In THE WIZARD OF OZ, Dorothy is asked pointblank, "Well, Dorothy, what did you learn?" And then Dorothy tells us all the ways her perceptions and attitudes have changed. Most important, her attitude toward home has changed. She realizes now that "there's no place like home."

At the end of CASABLANCA, Louie observes, "Rick, you've become a patriot."

In CITY SLICKERS, after Billy Crystal battles the river, he declares, "I know the meaning of life. It's my family."

When Holly Hunter goes overboard with the piano (in THE PIANO), she realizes she wants to live.

Oskar Schindler is presented with a ring at the end of SCHINDLER'S LIST. He realizes the good he's done and that maybe he is a good man after all.

In the beginning of FALLING DOWN, we identify with Michael Douglas, but soon lose affection for him as he declines. Robert Duvall, however, grows. So our affections shift to him. At the end, these two characters square off, both realizing what they've become. Robert Duvall has become a good cop and a man. Michael Douglas has a different realization. He says, "You mean I'm the bad guy?"

How does growth come about? Only through adversity and opposition, and striving for a goal. Only through conflict, making decisions, and taking actions. "True character is revealed," the proverb goes, "when you come face-to-face with adversity."

As a footnote, let me reiterate that in some action/adventures, thrillers, and other stories, the central character may not grow. James Bond doesn't grow; he just accomplishes his mission. However, in most genres, character growth of some sort is desirable, and even essential. One reason I enjoyed DIE HARD was that the writer gave action hero Bruce Willis room to grow in his relationship with his wife.

BELIEVABILITY

One reason dramatic characters are interesting is that they are generally single-minded and focused. Humans have more things going on in their lives and tend to run off on tangents. Your job as the next great screenwriter is to make your dramatic and comedic characters seem as human as possible. In other words, your job is to make us care about them. Here are some ways to accomplish that.

Give them human emotions

As you know, people watch movies to feel emotion vicariously. Whether it's love, revenge, fear, anticipation, or what-have-you, you can only touch these moviegoers if they are able to relate to how your character feels. This doesn't mean that your character should blubber all over the place but that we need to see your character in love, frustrated, hurt, scared, thrilled, etc.

RAIN MAN is a remarkable film because one of the main characters is incapable of emotionally connecting with another person. I admire the writers, who dealt with this problem by giving Dustin Hoffman a desire to drive a car. "I'm an excellent driver," he would say. If your eyes became misty, it was at the end, when Tom Cruise lets Hoffman drive the car on a circular driveway.

Give them human traits

First focus on the core of your character—her soul. Who is she? What is her strongest trait? It is important to identify this dominant trait. Then look for a flaw that might serve as a contrast, to create an inner conflict.

When SNOW WHITE AND THE SEVEN DWARFS was being developed, the dwarfs were seven old guys who looked alike and acted the same. Then Walt Disney decided to give each dwarf a human trait and to call him by that trait. What a difference a trait makes.

It is also important to include characteristics, problems, and imperfections that are familiar to all humans. He's a grouch. She can't deal with people until she's had her morning coffee. Inconsequential human imperfections will make your dramatic or comedic character more believable, more human.

Give them human values

Now let's take a moment to consider the Corleone family. It's doubtful that you'd invite these guys over for dinner. And yet, in the GODFATHER movies, you actually rooted for them. Why? Well, for one thing, these guys are loyal. They have a code of honor, a sense of justice. They have families and family values just like you and me. We like people with positive values.

If *your* central character happens to be a *bad guy*, make sure he's morally superior to the others in the story. If your character breaks the law, make him less corrupt than the law. The Corleones had a code of honor—they didn't sell drugs. Sure, extortion, protection rackets, murder, prostitution, gambling, but hey—they didn't sell drugs.

Other ways to create a little sympathy for your character is to give her a talent for what she does, and/or an endearing personal style in how she does it. Give her a moment alone to reveal her goodness. In such a moment, Rocky moves a wino out of the street and talks to a puppy.

Confront your character with an injustice, or place him in a difficult situation or in jeopardy. Be careful not to make him too much of a victim. In GODFATHER II, the Corleones are immigrants in an unfair situation. We sympathize. They take action. We may not agree with their choices, but we admire their fortitude.

Give them human dimension

Your characters, and particularly your central character, should have dimension. Avoid cardboard characters and stereotypes. Occasionally a stereotype works, particularly in a comedy or action script, but your main characters will play better if they have depth. No one is totally evil or perfectly good. The bad guy loves his cat, while the good guy kicks his dog once in a while.

Writers have a tendency to make their favorite characters flat, lifeless, and passive. We're afraid to bloody their face or to give them flaws. Don't fall into that trap. By and large, the most loved characters in film have depth and dimension. Yours should, too.

DETAILS

Details are the little things that mean a lot. Think of them as characterization tools or aspects of character. Idiosyncracies, habits, quirks, and other characterizations will add a lot to a character. They help make the character a distinct individual. What would Columbo be without his crumpled overcoat?

Personal expressions can make a difference. The Emperor in AMADEUS concludes his pronouncements with, "Well, there it is," and Raymond the Rainman says, "I'm an excellent driver." Holly Hunter just cries periodically in BROADCAST NEWS, and Roger Rabbit has an endearing way of stuttering when he says, "Please."

Give your character a specialized knowledge or skill, such as Matthew Broderick's computer-hacking skill in WAR GAMES, and Luke's knowledge of The Force in STAR WARS. In THREE DAYS OF THE CONDOR, Robert Redford is a full-time reader for the CIA. It's easy to believe in his intelligence and knowledge when he's forced to the streets.

Props have been used with good effect. Captain Quigg's ball bearings. Kojak's lollypop. Captain Hook's hook. James Bond's gadgets. Whenever Indiana Jones gets into trouble, he has his whip. He uses the whip to get himself out of trouble. (The whip, of course, does not save him. He uses the whip to save himself. That's an important distinction.)

It follows that coincidences should generally work against your central character. Make it increasingly difficult for her to achieve her goal. Don't bail her out at the end (*Deus ex machina*). She should be the most active character in the final act.

A WRITER WHO CARES

Every character hopes for a writer who cares. Your central character must have a life and a voice of his own. He can only get that from a writer who cares. You show that you care by researching.

The main purpose of research is to come to really know your characters. Once you know who they are, you can observe them emerging on the page as real. One of the most beautiful experiences you can have is when your characters take over your story and tell you what they want to do.

Research is observing people, taking notes in your little writer's notebook when things occur to you. Research is searching your mind, your own experience, people you've known who can serve as character prototypes, places you've seen, and so forth.

Research is investigating, exploring, and creating your character's background. For instance, your character has an educational background; ethnic, cultural, and religious roots; a professional (or work) history; past and present social connections; and a family of some kind. Your character also has a particular way of speaking.

What kind of character would Forrest Gump be if little thought were put to his background, psychology, traits, imperfections, idiosyncracies, and moral character?

Research is trips to the library for information, or to a place of business to understand your character's occupation. Research is interviewing someone of a particular ethnic group, or even visiting a neighborhood. Don't assume you can get by because you've seen other movies that have dealt with the same subject matter.

It's easy to get interviews. Recently, I interviewed a petroleum geologist. I told him I'd buy him lunch if he'd let me ask him some questions. He was thrilled for several reasons. One, he could tell the guys at work, "Hey, I can't go to lunch with you tomorrow. I got a writer interviewing me for an upcoming movie." Two, he was getting a free lunch. Three, he was proud of the job he does. The benefit to me was that I learned many things, unexpected things that I could use in my screenplay to lend authenticity and authority to it.

A struggling student on the East Coast tells me she didn't really understand her story until she interviewed a blackjack dealer in Las Vegas. Another from the heartland benefited immensely from a quick jaunt to the library to investigate fencing and other kinds of sword fighting.

Research is writing a character biography or completing a detailed character profile. Of course, much of this information will never make it into your script, but since your character will be alive to you, he or she will appear more fully drawn on the page.

Although your character's physical description is very important to you, it will be of little importance to the script. All actors want to see themselves in the part, so only include physical details that are essential to the story. When you describe a character in your script, it will be with a few lines or words that really give us the essence of the character. Something the actors can act.

But you, the writer, the creator, need to see this person in detail, because a person's physiology affects his psychology. What kinds of emotions does your character have? What is her disposition? How does he handle relationships?

Identify complexes, phobias, pet peeves, fears, secrets, attitudes, beliefs, addictions, prejudices, inhibitions, frustrations, habits, superstitions, and moral stands. Is your character extroverted or introverted, aggressive or passive, intuitive or analytical? How does he solve problems? How does she deal with stress? An so on. Have fun with this!

Research is reflecting, and asking questions.

- What are my character's values?
- What does my character do when she is all alone?
- What's the most traumatic thing that ever happened to my character?
- What is his biggest secret?
- What is her most poignant moment?
- What are his hobbies?
- What special abilities does she have?
- What is his deepest fear?
- What kind of underwear does she wear?
- Which end of the toothpaste tube does he squeeze? (Well, you don't have to go that far, although it's not hard to guess which end Felix Unger squeezes.)
- What is the worst thing that could happen to my character?
- What is the best thing that could happen?
- What is my character doing tonight?

Research is creating unique aspects to your character that makes her stand apart from all other movie characters. Part of this may be giving your character a contradiction or traits that exist in opposition, such as the beautiful woman who's as clumsy as an ox, or Brave Indiana Jones' fear of snakes. You may wish to identify one or more loveable imperfections as well.

As this research progresses, certain things will stand out. After all, in the actual script, you will only be able to emphasize certain aspects of your character, so you will want to select those that say the most about your character and relate the best to your story. The work you've done will reveal itself in the unique and multi-faceted character that you have created from the dust.

When do you do this research? Some writers like to do it early in the process; others prefer later in the writing so the characters can be created to fit the demands of the script. Most need to be thorough with this. A thumbnail sketch of the main characters is seldom sufficient.

A STRONG SUPPORTING CAST

A screenplay is a symphony and a symphony requires orchestration. Your character is just a lonely solo without other characters. Obviously, you'll want to do some thinking here as well. In the well-written story, relationships are emphasized. Some relationships work because of opposite personalities. The ODD COUPLE is an excellent example.

Some because each can fill the other's need and they transform each other. Some relationships work because the characters are rivals. Some work because of similar interests or goals.

In your cast of characters, you want one central character, at least one opposition character, and a confidant (or sidekick) whom your central character can talk to. This is one way to reveal your central character's thoughts, feelings, and intentions. The confidant sometimes performs the additional function of lending contrast to your central character. The opposition character does not have to be a villain. There is no villain in KRAMER VS. KRAMER. And even villains are not usually evil in their own eyes.

You will probably want a love interest, who may function in another role as well.

Occasionally, you see a thematic character, someone who carries the theme or message of the story, such as the mathematician in JURASSIC PARK.

You want characters with contrasts, and you can contrast characters on many levels, from attitudes to methods to social status. As you add characters, remember that each character in your story must perform a specific function in moving the story forward.

Note: This is a good time to do Step 4 in the workbook (Book III).

Dialogue, subtext, and exposition

WHAT DIALOGUE IS

Dialogue is not real-life speech; it only sounds like it. It is more focused, less rambling than real-life speech. Yes, it contains fragments and short bits, but anything extraneous is pulled out, including the *ans* and *uhs*. You might say that dialogue is *edited* speech. It is organized and has direction, but it retains the style of real-life speech.

Dialogue should be lean and short. Avoid long speeches. Try to keep to one or two lines. Remember that in a movie, people have to understand what's being said the first time through. In a novel, a passage can be reread, but a movie keeps "reeling" along.

Take a look at your script and ask yourself: Is there a better, leaner way to say this? Am I writing more but the audience enjoying it less? I'm not saying you can't write long speeches; I'm only saying they must be justifiable.

Be patient in writing dialogue. Sometimes it takes a while for your dialogue to break through. With many professional writers, dialogue is often the last thing written, so don't panic if your dialogue isn't working at first. The key here is to know your characters well enough that they speak with a voice of their own. That voice consists of eight elements.

     1. The text, or words
     2. The subtext, or the meaning of the words
     3. Grammar and syntax
     4. Vocabulary
     5. Accent and/or regional or foreign influences
     6. Slang
     7. Professional jargon
     8. Speaking style, including rhythm and sentence length.

IT'S NOT WHAT YOU SAY, BUT HOW YOU SAY IT

Mama was right—the subtext (how you say it) has more impact that the text. Of the eight elements of dialogue, subtext is the one that gives writers the most fits.

What is subtext? Subtext is what's under the text. It's between the lines, the emotional content of the words, what's really meant. When an actor wants to know her motivation in a scene, she wants to understand the emotions going on within the character. She wants to know the subtext.

Usually, the dialogue's context in the story suggests the subtext. For example, in the "fireworks" scene of TO CATCH A THIEF, Grace Kelly seduces Cary Grant, a reformed jewel thief. That's the context. Does she talk about sex? Does she say, "Come on, Cary, let's go for a roll in the hay?" Of course not. This moment requires finesse. She talks about her jewelry, and wouldn't he do anything to steal such beautiful works of art? "Hold them," she says, "the one thing you can't resist." Clearly, she's not talking about jewelry here. The subtext is, "I'm the jewelry, you're the thief—take me." She says one thing by saying something else. The subtext is always obvious to the audience.

In a previous section, we discussed goals and needs—your character not only has an outside goal but some inner need. The goal is the *text* of the story and the need may be thought of as the *subtext* of the story, or emotional through-line. It follows, therefore, that the subtext of the dialogue in a scene will often derive from the character's underlying need or drive in the scene.

In MOONLIGHTING, a woman hires David and Maddy to find her runaway husband. David and Maddy then argue over the motives of the husband for running away. What are they really talking about? Their own relationship. It's more fun to listen to them when they are indirect.

Subtext has to do with the true intention of the character. The PRINCESS BRIDE is the story of a grandfather who wants to convert his young grandson to a kissing book. A kissing book is one where the boy and the girl actually kiss in the end—yuk! The grandson is sick in bed and is forced to listen to his grandfather read him this kissing book. The grandfather begins reading something like this:

"Once upon a time, there was a boy and a girl. And the girl used to torture the boy by asking him to do things for her, and every time the girl asked the boy to do something for her, he would say, 'As you wish.' But what he was really saying when he said *as you wish* was *I love you*."

I can't think of a better explanation of the relationship between the spoken word and the subtext than this grandfather's explanation.

At the end of this movie, the grandson is converted to this kissing book—he likes it— and as the grandfather leaves, the boy asks him if he could . . . well maybe . . . come by tomorrow and read it again. And the grandfather says, "As you wish." Wouldn't you agree that this indirect statement, loaded with subtext, is much more powerful than the more direct *I love you*? And it's a lot more fun as well.

Which works better? *I'm very fond of you, Ilsa*. Or: "Here's looking at you, kid."

Here's a dramatic situation: A cop confronts a robber who holds his gun to an innocent woman's head. Which line works better? *If you shoot her, I'll be real glad, because I'm gonna enjoy killing you*. Or: "Go ahead, make my day." In this case, less is more.

When writing dialogue, keep in mind the character's attitudes, point of view, feelings, thoughts, and underlying need or drive. Try to say one thing by saying something else. This does not mean that every line of dialogue must have a subtext. However, most beginning scripts have too little subtext.

WRITING BETTER DIALOGUE

Here's a technique that will improve your dialogue. Read your dialogue out loud or have members of your writers' group read it to you. With the spoken word, it's easier to detect errors. You will hear what works and what doesn't. Is the dialogue too *on the nose*, too direct? without an implied meaning or subtext?

Also be aware of the rhythm. Some characters are terse and staccato; some are lyrical and elegant. Each character has a style of speech. Avoid VOICE OVER narration. Avoid chitchat. *Hi, how are you? Fine, and how about you?* Also, avoid introductions. *Hi, this is Clark. Clark, this is Lois.* In the well-written story, when introductions are made, there's some clear and overriding dramatic purpose. It's not just cheap exposition.

Dialogue should also move the story forward, just as scenes do, and reveal something about the character's attitudes, perceptions, and values. Every dialogue scene should involve some conflict, even if it is just passive resistance. Back and forth, like a contest or competition.

In FIVE EASY PIECES, Jack Nicholson stops at a diner. He wants toast, he orders toast, but the waitress won't give him toast because it's not on the menu. He tries several approaches. She fends him off every time, each time the tension building, the conflict escalating. Finally he orders a chicken salad sandwich, toasted. And tells her to hold the butter, lettuce, and mayonnaise, and to hold the chicken between her knees. She kicks him out, so he clears everything off the table and onto the floor. The exchange of verbal blows creates the rising tension of this classic scene.

EXCITING EXPOSITION

Another purpose of dialogue is to communicate the necessary facts of the story. These facts are called *exposition*. Your job is to make the exposition exciting.

Most of the exposition comes out in the beginning of the story. For example, the audience needs to understand how Indiana Jones' mission will benefit the world. Don't give the audience any more information than necessary to understand the story. Be careful not to reveal too much too soon. Let your characters keep their secrets as long as they can. Often, saving up exposition and using it in crucial moments will make it more exciting, and even transform it into a turning point. Do you remember, for example, when Darth Vader said, "Luke, I am your father."?

Some exposition can be creatively planted in love scenes, action scenes, or comedy scenes, because at those moments you already have the audience's attention. In any case, the exposition should come forth naturally and not be tacked onto a scene. Seldom should you allow one character to tell the other something he already knows: *We've been married ten years now, honey.*

Be careful not to get *too* exciting. In the second INDIANA JONES movie, the main exposition is presented through dialogue at a bizarre dinner. The food is so disgusting that the audience's attention is diverted from the characters' dialogue.

In the first INDIANA JONES movie, the exposition is handled more effectively. The opening sequence is so exciting that we are riveted to the screen for the succeeding sequence, where most of the necessary information about the Lost Ark of the Covenant is communicated through dialogue.

Another way to make exposition exciting is to have characters argue over it, as in FLATLINERS. Some exposition can be handled without dialogue. This is even better. In the opening sequence of WAR GAMES, we are shown how the U.S. nuclear-missile firing system works. This information not only underscores the danger and prepares us for a thrilling ending, but also makes the story more believable.

Flashbacks

About ninety-five percent of the flashbacks in unsold scripts doesn't work. Usually, the flashback is used as a crutch, a cheap way to introduce exposition. This has given rise to the industry bias against them in spec scripts. Seldom does it move the story forward. And that's the key—use a flashback only if it moves the story forward. Don't give exposition in a flashback unless it also motivates the story, as in JULIA and CASABLANCA. Do not take us to the past until we care about what's happening in the future. Otherwise, a flashback becomes an interruption.

Avoid long flashbacks and dream sequences. They are high-risk. If you must have a flashback, use a transitional device: an object, place, song, visual image, color, phrase, or incident. Quick flashes are the safest, such as the momentary glimpses of the backstory we see in ORDINARY PEOPLE.

My advice on flashbacks is to find a more creative way to communicate exposition. To illustrate, put yourself in the place of the writer of STAR TREK II: THE WRATH OF KHAN. You have a problem: Khan, the opposition character, is Kirk's superior physically and mentally. How can you make it believable that Kirk can defeat Khan?

One solution is to *flash back* to the days when Kirk was a cadet. He takes a field test called the Kobiashi Maru, which presents a no-win scenario. Kirk, however, beats the no-win scenario by re-programming the test computer so that he can win.

You, however, reject this idea of a flashback for one that is more creative. You decide to open the story with a starfleet captain on a ship that is in trouble. Soon we learn that this captain is really a cadet and that she is taking a test called the Kobiashi Maru. She is bothered by her performance. Kirk tells her not to worry, that there is no correct solution—it's a test of character. So she asks Kirk how *he* handled it. He won't tell her.

You have made it a mystery that is touched on throughout the story—how *did* Kirk handle the Kobiashi Maru? The audience wonders. You, the next great screenwriter (and an adept one at that), have created suspense.

CUT TO: Late in the story. It appears as though Kirk and his friends are trapped in an underground cavern with no way out, and with no apparent way to contact Spock, who is somewhere in the universe. At that moment, the female cadet (who ran a Boston bar in a previous life) once again asks Kirk how he handled the Kobiashi Maru. Bones tells her that Kirk reprogrammed the computer. "You cheated," someone says.

Then Kirk surprises everyone by pulling out his communicator and contacting Spock: "You can beam us up now," he says. Ah-ha, so Kirk had it all pre-arranged. He has cheated Khan and has surprised everyone else. That's when Kirk explains: "I don't believe in the no-win scenario. I don't like to lose." Not only have you explained how Kirk could defeat a superior being, you have also given us the *key* to Kirk's character. And this plays much better than a flashback.

Theme

Did you know there is something inside you that is motivating you to write? There is something that you want to say. This thing inside you is not a little alien creature, it is the *movie message*, sometimes called *theme*. Regardless of what it is called, think of it as the *moral* of your story. This moral is not a sermon and it is not preached. Often, you don't know what this moral or message is when you start scripting your story. Not to worry—you'll know before you're through. Just keep writing. CAUTION: There is a danger in focusing on the movie message. You run the risk of writing a preachy script.

The resolution of your story will verify the acceptability of your message. This message could be expressed as a universal statement that could apply to anyone. It's something you've been wanting to say. For this reason, it can be thought of as the *point of view* of your story.

WITNESS has a point of view. *Love cannot bridge the gap of two different worlds.* In THE AFRICAN QUEEN, the opposite is true. *Love **can** bridge the gap of two different worlds.* As you can see, the movie message isn't necessarily true in real life, just true in your story. And it should never be communicated in a heavy-handed way.

The message of CHINATOWN is this: *You can get away with murder if you have enough money.*

WHEN HARRY MET SALLY suggests that *men and women cannot be "just friends."*

Times are a-changin', and you have to change with them if you want to survive. This thematic statement, or movie message, suggests characters who are fighting time (the conflict) and who will not succeed. Can you name the movie? BUTCH CASSIDY AND THE SUNDANCE KID.

Now there's also *thematic material*. For example, WITNESS explores themes of violence and nonviolence. BROADCAST NEWS presents substance vs. style.

In a few stories, it may be effective to create a thematic or symbolic character: someone whose purpose is to carry a theme, a value, or even the story message. This character is seldom the central character.

How to make a scene

Screenplays are composed of acts, acts break down into sequences, sequences into scenes, and scenes into beats. A scene is a dramatic unit consisting of the camera placement (INTERIOR or EXTERIOR), a location, and time. When one of these three elements changes, the scene changes as well. In this discussion, I am using the term *scene* loosely. The points that follow could apply to any dramatic unit consisting of one or more scenes.

KEYS TO GREAT SCENES

- Each scene should move the story forward in terms of both plot and character. In other words, the scene you are now writing should be motivated by a previous scene, and it should motivate a scene coming up. One creates anticipation for another in a cause-and-effect relationship.

  If the central character gets more involved in some way, that means your scene is probably moving the story forward. All scenes should direct us to the Showdown at the end, which is the biggest scene, or sequence of scenes, in the movie. Ask yourself: What is the payoff for this scene? Why do I need this scene? What is my purpose for this scene? At the end of this scene, does the audience want to know what happens next?

- Never tell what you can show. Be as visual as possible. Rather than two ladies at tea commenting on the fact that Darla skydives for relaxation, *show* us Darla actually jumping from a plane, or show her coming home with a parachute and trying to stuff it into the closet.

  Do you recall the barn-raising scene in WITNESS? When the workers pause for lunch, the eyes of the elders are on Kelly McGillis, who is expected to marry an Amish man, but who likes Harrison Ford. Without a word of dialogue, she makes her choice by pouring water for Harrison Ford first.

- Avoid talking heads. John and Mary argue over breakfast. One head talks, then the other. Make this more interesting by beginning the argument at breakfast, continuing it while in the car racing to the club, and concluding it during a racquetball match. Each statement a character makes is punctuated by the whack of the racket or the whop of the ball slamming against the wall. Now the action complements the dialogue.

- Every dramatic unit has a beginning, a middle, and an end. Yes, some scenes are short and transitional, but they are the exceptions.

- Start the scene as close to the end of the scene as possible. In other words, once your scene is fleshed out, evaluate it and lop off anything at the beginning that is unnecessary. (In fact, cut the fat anywhere you can.)

Imagine a cowboy riding up to a log house in the middle of the prairie. No one for miles around. He quietly dismounts, grabs his rifle, and gingerly approaches the cabin. He peeks through the window. There she is. Young, beautiful, and alone. Inside the cabin, the woman turns. The door is kicked in. The cowboy steps inside and points his rifle right at the woman. He wants the money and he wants her. She reaches behind for a knife and throws it at the cowboy.

Does this scene remind you of the opening scene of ROMANCING THE STONE? It is, except the final version of the scene begins at the moment the door is kicked in. Everything preceding that moment was cut. The writer started the scene as close to the end of the scene as possible.

In terms of scene length, challenge any scene that runs over two pages. Many great scenes are long, and some scenes should be long. Nevertheless, if you challenge your long scenes, you may find ways to improve them and shorten them. This will strengthen the pace of the story.

- Pace your scenes. Provide peaks and valleys of emotion and tension, with the peaks ascending toward a climatic conclusion. Follow action scenes with dialogue scenes. Contrast heavy scenes with light scenes. Make sure the pace quickens as you close in on the Crisis and Showdown. In HOME ALONE, we have the reflective scene in the church just before the madcap slapstick sequence at the house.

Pacing does not need to focus on action and events, such as in LETHAL WEAPON; it can focus on details as in STEEL MAGNOLIAS.

- Scenes should culminate in something dramatic. This could be a decision or an imminent decision. It could be a reversal, a cliffhanger, or a revelation—some event that makes us want to see what's going to happen next. Keep in mind that twists and turns in the plot are essential. You cannot allow your story to progress the way your audience expects it to. In dialogue scenes, end on a punch line, on something strong.

• Strive to create effective transitions between scenes. I'm not referring to tricky cuts and arty dissolves—leave editing directions to the editor. Find ways to fit the scenes together. For example, one scene ends with a roulette wheel spinning. The next scene begins with a car wheel digging into the mud.

Early in 2001: A SPACE ODYSSEY, a prehistoric man throws his tool into the air. It's a bone that becomes a spaceship, a tool of modern man.

Transitions can be visual, verbal, thematic, and so on. Is it okay to sharply contract scenes? Absolutely. If it moves the story forward, use it. Keep in mind that a straight cut from one scene to the next is fine. The object is not to get fancy but to give the story cohesion.

• Each scene should contain a definite emotion or mood. Focus on that emotion as you craft the scene. Ask yourself: What is my character's intention or goal in this scene? What is my character's feeling? What is my character's attitude? Asking this will help give the scene direction and the dialogue subtext.

• Focus the scene on a well-motivated conflict. Even in less dramatic scenes, a conflict should exist, regardless of how minor or how subtle it is. Often, two people with the same goal will disagree over methods or procedure, or just get under the other's skin: Bones and Spock, James Bond and Q, Butch Cassidy and Sundance. Even in love scenes, there may be some resistance at the beginning. Conflict is one of the tools you can use to build suspense.

Suspense, comedy, and television

Building suspense is the art of creating an expectation of something dramatic that is about to happen. Since we go to movies to feel emotion vicariously, putting us in suspense simply builds emotion as we anticipate the outcome. Here are ten tools to thrill and manipulate us.

TOOLS FOR BUILDING SUSPENSE

Evoke emotion

Create characters we like. They must be believable since they act as a conduit through which emotion can pass to us. We need to sympathize with them and feel what they feel.

Create conflict

As mentioned earlier, rising conflict creates suspense. Since conflict is drama, two committed forces in conflict will always heighten suspense. Remember grade school? Two boys would start fighting and everyone would make a circle around them. No one tried to stop the fight. (This is very irritating if you're the smaller boy.) No one stopped it because we were all in suspense, wondering if blood would squirt out someone's nose, and betting on who would win.

Provide opposition

Give your central character *a powerful opposition*; then force your character to battle this foe. The opposition should be in a position of strength, capable of doing damage. In STAR TREK II, Khan serves as an excellent example, because he is superior to Kirk physically and mentally. We all go through the extreme mental duress of wondering how Kirk is going to survive, let alone defeat, this "giant." The "giant" in FATAL ATTRACTION is Glenn Close, the lover. She is in a position to do damage to Michael Douglas.

Build expectation

Create an *expectation for trouble.* Do you recall the baby carriage in THE UNTOUCH-ABLES? In this scene, Elliot Ness must face off with Capone's boys at the train station. He's ready and in position, but a woman is having difficulty moving her baby carriage up the stairs. We get nervous—we just "know" she is going to get in the way. The suspense builds.

Consider also the scene from FATAL ATTRACTION where Michael Douglas returns home and finds his wife conversing with his lover. There is an expectation that the wife might realize that this blonde she is talking to is actually a woman who is having an affair with her husband. In this case the jeopardy is emotional, not physical.

Increase Tension

Put the audience in a *superior position.* Take, for example, a couple we care about. While they are out to dinner, someone sneaks into their apartment and places a bomb under their bed. Later, our happy couple returns and they hop into bed. *We* know the bomb is there, but they don't. We, the audience, are in a superior position.

Imagine a small child playing in the yard. The mother steps inside the house. The child wanders toward the busy street. We are in a superior position to the child *and* to the mother. We are the only ones who are aware of the danger, and that builds suspense.

Use surprise

Throw in an occasional nasty twist, or sudden turn of events. Do you recall WAIT UNTIL DARK? Remember Alan Arkin leaping from the shadows at Audrey Hepburn? You couldn't hear the rest of the movie for all the screaming in the theater.

In PSYCHO, Hitchcock kills Janet Leigh early in the now-famous shower scene. This nasty twist serves the purpose of creating an expectation of *more* violence. Indeed, Hitchcock once remarked, "At this point I transferred the horror from the screen to the minds of the audience." Interestingly enough, there is only one more violent act in the entire movie, and yet we are held in suspense throughout.

Create immediacy

When *something vital is at stake* for the character, that *something* becomes vital to us, the audience, as well. It can be the physical safety of the world or the moral redemption of a juvenile delinquent. It can be the emotional fulfillment of two lovers who find each other, the protection of a secret document, or the triumph of a value. The higher the stakes, the more intense the suspense.

Establish consequences

Closely related to the above is the establishment of terrible consequences if the central character does not achieve her goal. When the Challenger space shuttle exploded, there was a lot of grief and sadness. A couple of years later, we sent up another shuttle. Do you recall the suspense you felt as the countdown proceeded on this later shuttle mission? That heightened suspense was due to the prior establishment of terrible consequences.

Limit time

Put a ticking clock on it. "You have only twenty-four hours to save the world, James. Good luck." Deadlines, such as the one in THE PAPER, create suspense because they introduce an additional opposition—time. You can probably think of a dozen movies where a bomb is about to explode, and the hero must defuse it before the countdown reaches zero. The torpedo-firing sequences in THE HUNT FOR RED OCTOBER were particularly thrilling because of the element of time.

Likewise, when the wicked witch in THE WIZARD OF OZ captures Dorothy, she turns over the hour glass. "This is how long you have to live, my little pretty." Although we are never told how Dorothy is going to die, we still worry. Apparently, Hitchcock was right when he said that "the threat of violence is stronger than violence."

You can easily create an artificial deadline. The damsel is tied to the railroad tracks. Can Dudley Do-right save the damsel before the train runs over her? Here you have an implied deadline. Other effective uses of the ticking clock include HIGH NOON and the rose petals in Disney's BEAUTY AND THE BEAST.

Maintain doubt

Finally, if there is a reasonable doubt about how the scene or movie is going to end, the suspense is intensified. In the opening scene of THE UNTOUCHABLES, one of Capone's boys leaves a briefcase full of explosives in a store. A little girl picks it up and it explodes. At this point, we realize that anyone in this movie can die, and we fret over Elliot Ness's little girl and wife the entire movie. Why? Because there is genuine doubt about their safety.

LEAVE 'EM LAUGHING

Have you ever watched a comedy and laughed for about twenty minutes and then grown restless? The probable reason for this is that the comedy had a weak story structure with poorly drawn characters. The comedy may have relied more on gags than on character and story.

Comedy is drama in disguise. And there is no comedy without conflict. That means virtually everything in this book applies to comedy as well as to drama. Here are a few points that apply particularly to comedy.

Comedy requires clarity and good timing—a *sense* of humor.

Comedy situations are easy for people to relate to. That's one reason the family situation comedy has done so well.

Comedy makes good use of surprise and reversals.

Comedy generally takes an unusual point of view through use of exaggeration, deception, overstatement, understatement, contrast, parody, a ridiculous point of view, or obsession.

Comedy presents people with pretenses or façades, then removes them little by little. One scene from PLAY IT AGAIN, SAM features Woody Allen preparing for a blind date (a situation we can all relate to—right?). He goes to extremes to impress her. He thinks he can score the first night, and that's his pretense. He impresses her, all right, but not the way he had hoped. It's a reversal of what he expected. He's brought back to earth.

TELEVISION

As you can imagine, television comedy writing is less visual than screenwriting, with less action. There may be only one or two locations. And so the emphasis is on interpersonal conflict and dialogue. The best situation for a sitcom is one that forces the characters to be together. M*A*S*H, NIGHT COURT, ROSEANNE, FRASIER, and THE SIMPSONS are examples.

Sitcoms thrive with a *gang of four*, four main characters where each can easily be at cross-purposes with any of the others, creating more possibilities for conflict. In other words, they can play off each other.

Structurally, the sitcom opens with a teaser that says, "Boy, this is going to be really funny. Don't change the channel during the next two minutes of commercials!" Act 1 introduces the secondary storyline and the primary storyline in succession. (Sometimes one of these is introduced in the teaser.) Act 1 ends on a turning point that is either the most hilarious moment in the episode, or is very serious. The second act resolves the primary story, then the secondary story. This is followed by a tag at the end that usually comments on the resolution. SEINFELD usually presents three stories or plot lines.

The hour-long TV drama or comedy also opens with a teaser or prologue. Act 1 establishes what's going on, Acts 2 and 3 develop it, Act 4 pays it off. Most shows add an epilogue. If the show is relationship-driven, an arena is created in which the story can play. The arena for MOONLIGHTING is a detective agency.

The *long form*, or Movie-of-the-Week (MOW), contains seven acts and about 105 pages. That means six turning points must be carefully planned. It might be simpler to write this as a screenplay. In fact, the best way to break into television of any kind is with a feature script that you can use as a sample. It shows you can create characters from scratch and write a story around them. Being the next great screenwriter, it's a challenge you can meet.

Note: This is a good time to do Step 5 in the workbook (Book III). Next, read the formatting and style guide (Book II). Then do Steps 6 and 7 in the workbook. Finally, use the marketing plan in Book IV to sell your screenplay, consulting the resources in Book V.

CORRECT FORMAT FOR SCREENPLAYS & TELEPLAYS

BOOK II

A Style Guide for Spec Scripts

How to use this guide
and its unique cross-referencing tools

This book gives you everything you need to know and only what you need to know to correctly format your screenplay or teleplay. It also teaches you about writing and writing *style*. Every attempt has been made to simplify the material.

Professional scripts sometimes vary slightly in formatting style, and yet they all look basically the same—they all look like scripts. There are surprisingly few absolutes. These formatting guidelines are like accounting principles—they are generally accepted by the industry. They will increase your script's chances of being accepted by agents, producers, directors, and talent (actors and actresses).

This book is both a textbook and a reference book. It contains clear, how-to instructions and sample scenes. You can easily find information in any of the following ways.

1. Use the **index** (pages 101-103) to quickly find any subject area or term.

2. Read the **body of the text** (pages 66-99) as a style guide. It consists of numerous how-to instructions and explanations, which are easily spotted. Most are also identified by a letter code. This letter *reference code* can be cross-referenced to the same reference code in the sample scenes on pages 63-65. For example, on page 88 in the body of the text, you will find reference code [T] next to an explanation of OFF SCREEN. Using that reference code, you can cross-reference to page 65, where you will find the same reference code [T] next to an example of OFF SCREEN in the sample scenes.

3. Read the **sample scenes** on pages 63-65 and, using the same coding system explained in Number 2 above, cross-reference to an explanation in the body of the text. These codes appear in alphabetical order in the body of the text.

4. Note how the guidelines are grouped, and then go to specific areas that you need to study.

5. Check the glossary on page 100 for terms not defined anywhere else.

Some writers may wish to mark the first page of the index with a paper clip for fast access. The first page of the sample scene could also be marked with a paper clip.

All sample scenes and excerpts appear just as they would in an actual script, right down to the 10-pitch, 12-point font (see pages 67-68). One last thing to keep in mind before going on—you are writing a *spec* script (on *spec*ulation that you will sell it later).

THE *SPEC* SCRIPT—HOW IT IS DIFFERENT

The *spec* script is the *selling* script. You write it with the idea of selling it later or circulating it as a sample. (Once it is sold, it will be transformed into a *shooting* script.) The *spec*-script style avoids camera angles, editing directions, and technical intrusions. You may use these tools, but only when absolutely necessary to clarify the story. Scenes are not numbered in the spec script; that's done by the production secretary after your script is sold.

All the camera and editing directions in the world cannot save a bad story, but too much technical intrusion can make even the best story a chore to read. The main reason you write a *spec* script is to tell an interesting story. So concentrate on the story and leave the direction to the director and the editing to the editor.

Virtually every script you buy from a script service or bookstore, or view in a script library, is a *shooting* script, or a variation thereof. Most screenwriting books contain formatting instructions for *shooting* scripts only. To make matters worse, some professional writers, producers, and even agents still recommend the *shooting* script format because it's what they've always used and it's what working writers use when they are hired to write directly for a production.

But the *shooting* script is not a joy to read for agents, executives, and readers who must plow through dozens of scripts every week, week after week. The technical directions clutter the script and intrude on the reading experience. That's fine if the script is about to be produced, but it works against you if you want your story to flow smoothly to the reader, enticing him/her to buy or recommend it to the higher-ups.

Both script styles utilize the same basic formatting rules—master scene headings in CAPS, double-space to narrative description, dialogue indented, and so on. And the *spec* script occasionally employs some *shooting* script terms: MONTAGE, FLASH-BACK, INSERT for notes and letters, and INTERCUT for telephone conversations.

The essential difference between the two styles is this: The *shooting* script format requires specific technical instructions so that the director, crew, and cast can more easily perform in the shoot. The *spec* script format emphasizes clear, unencumbered visual writing to sell agents and producers on a great story.

What follows is a sample of a title page (page 62) and sample scenes (pages 63-65) in correct format with the cross-referencing codes mentioned earlier. These are followed by pages of explanations and instruction, which often provide alternate examples. After all, there is usually more than one way to apply the formatting guidelines. Last is a glossary and a complete formatting index.

A personal note: In response to the many owners of past editions of this guidebook who have written me concerning the content of the sample scenes that follow, I now feel compelled to explain that the scenes romanticize my teaching policy of tossing a candy mint to any student who makes a brilliant comment or asks a profound question. Yes, now it can be told, I am the perspicacious professor.

THE PERSPICACIOUS PROFESSOR

by

David R. Trottier

2034 East Lincoln #300
Anaheim, CA 92806
(714) 251-1073

62

FADE IN: [A]
                    [F]
A large university campus. Walkways are jammed with students. A
sign on a building reads: "CINEMA DEPARTMENT."   [K]

          [C]
INT. SMALL CLASSROOM - DAY   [B]

Twenty students sit in rapt attention while a handsome PROFESSOR
[I] scrawls "FORMATTING" across the blackboard. Slung over his
shoulder is a leather pouch, the kind used by Sea World trainers,
only this one is filled with candy mints instead of fish.
     [I]
CHARLIE, kicking back near a window, suddenly throws his hand up.
His face is covered with freckles and peanut butter. Two BUZZING
[L] flies vie for territorial rights to the peanut butter.

                    CHARLIE
          How do you handle phone calls?

The professor moonwalks to Charlie's desk carrying a demo phone.

          [R]   PROFESSOR
          Excellent question, my man.

He tosses the grateful boy a candy mint. Charlie catches it on
his nose and BARKS like a seal.   [M]

Outside Charlie's window, a YOUNG WOMAN in pigtails and a   [G]
pinafore yanks someone out of the phone booth and steps in.

          [C]
EXT. CLASSROOM - DAY   [H]
                    [J]
The young woman is CALCUTTA COTTER. With the phone to her ear,
she turns toward the classroom window and frowns at what she sees
-- the professor doing cartwheels down the aisle.   [G]

                    WOMAN'S VOICE (on phone)   [U]
          Make him pay, Calcutta.

INTERCUT - CALCUTTA AND DEAN ZACK TELEPHONE CONVERSATION   [V]

The voice belongs to DEAN ZELDA ZACK who stands at her desk with
a swagger stick tucked under her arm. Her polished desk is bare
except for a large metal sign that says, "DEAN, CINEMA DEPARTMENT."

                    CALCUTTA
          It'll work?

                    DEAN ZACK
          Stumps him every time.

The dean chortles. Calcutta smiles, then SLAMS the receiver.

                                                            63

INT. CLASSROOM - DAY
                    [N]
The professor's hand SLAMS the receiver of his demonstrator
phone. The students simmer with interest.

Quietly, the classroom door opens. Calcutta steps in and
shuffles to her desk as the professor expounds.

                         PROFESSOR
     [W]   Remember. It's gotta be lean.
          Description...dialogue.
                    (arching his brow)
          All lean, my pets -- lean!

He pirouettes and clicks his heels, accepting the rapturous
glances of his disciples.

                         CALCUTTA
          I wanna know something.

A hush fades into silence. When she speaks again, her lips are
not unlike those of Orson Welles when he said, "Rosebud."

                         CALCUTTA   **[S]**
          The _tabs_. Where do I set them?

The professor wilts under the heat of Calcutta's challenge. The
students exchange questioning glances as the professor stumbles
dizzily to his desk. He gazes blankly ahead, in a trance, and
watches the room spin around him. **[O]**

MONTAGE - THE PROFESSOR'S TRANCE **[D]**

The room spins. He jabs at a giant tab key on a keyboard to no
effect. In frustration, he hurls the computer out the window.
Instantly, Dean Zelda Zack rides up to the same window on her
swagger stick. He recoils. She transforms into a witch,
CACKLES, and rides off. The spinning room slows to a stop. **[M]**

BACK TO CLASSROOM

The students are horrified. Calcutta smiles gleefully. The
professor looks like he's just been hit by a Scud missile.

                         CHARLIE
          Our dear professor. What's wrong?

                         PROFESSOR
          Where to set your...tabs?

Several students clench the edges of their desks. Can he do it?
[P]

                    CHARLIE (OS)   **[T]**
         He's done for.

Murmurs of agreement. The professor stares at his shoes and makes
an attempt at moonwalking. His feet start remembering.

                    PROFESSOR
         Where to set your tabs. Assume
         a left margin at...at fifteen.

The students brighten in their seats. Calcutta frowns. The
professor is now in a serious moonwalking stride.

                    PROFESSOR
           (the master)
         Dialogue at...um...twenty-five.
         Parentheticals at thirty-one...

The students lean forward in their seats, all at exactly the same
angle, all but Calcutta, who nervously chews a pigtail.

                    PROFESSOR **[S]**
         ...And then the character's name
         -- in caps! -- at thirty-seven!

Cheers and kudos. The professor's moonwalk has taken him to
Calcutta's desk, where he towers over her limp form.

                    PROFESSOR
         But why, Calcutta? Why?

                    CALCUTTA
         Cuz everyone else always gets a
         candy, even Charlie, and I don't.

Her shoulders heave in heavy sobs.

INSERT - THE PROFESSOR'S POUCH **[E]**

His fingers deftly lift a candy mint.

BACK TO SCENE **[E]**

Calcutta lifts her head just as he flicks the candy into the air.
She catches it on her nose, BARKS like a seal, and consumes it
greedily. The students cheer. As the professor pats her head,
her pigtails rise as if to extend her radiant smile.

The cover, title page, front page, and last page

OVERALL SCREENPLAY APPEARANCE

Physically, a screenplay consists of a front cover (of solid color index stock, at least 65 pound, preferably 110 pound), a title page (or *fly page*), the pages of the script itself (printed on one side only), and a back cover—all 8½" x 11", all three-hole punched. That's it. Nothing appears on the front cover, not even the title. Your script will be placed on a stack. Someone will write your title on the side binding with a magic marker. Don't do it for them.

To bind the script together, use Acco (or some other brand) No. 5 round-head brass fasteners, 1¼" in length. (Some people like to use No. 6 or No. 7.) It is fashionable to place the fasteners (or "brads") in the first and third hole and leave the middle hole empty. Do not bind a script in any other way. The above method makes it easy for producers and others excited about your work to make photocopies to pass around, which is something you want.

Here's a list of NO-NOs in preparing your script for submission to agents:

- No fancy covers or artwork on the inside.
- Don't number the scenes. This is done after the script is sold.
- No fancy fonts or proportional fonts, only 12-point Courier or PICA. See page 67.
- No justified right margins. See page 68.
- Don't use a dot-matrix printer. Photocopies are okay.
- Don't date your script in any way. Scripts get old fast.
- Don't write "First Draft," "Final Draft," or any draft.
- No suggested cast list or character list with bios, unless requested.
- Don't include a list of characters or sets.
- Don't include a synopsis unless requested—you are selling your ability to write.
- Don't include a budget.

Your script should be 100-120 pages. Don't go over 120 pages. Don't cheat by using thinner margins, by squeezing more on a page, by using a smaller typeface, or by lengthening dialogue lines.

The above rules may seem picky, but they're easy to comply with, and adhering to them places you in the realm of the professional writer in the know.

THE TITLE PAGE

The example you see on page 62 is correct for a script that has not yet found an agent. Nothing else belongs on the page. You may add quotation marks around the title if you wish, or underscore it. If there are two writers and the two worked together and contributed equally, use an *ampersand* instead of the word *and*. For example:

"NAZIS IN SPACE"

by

Bart Snarf & Buffy Taylor

When the word *and* is used, it usually means a writer was brought in later to rewrite the first writer's script.

Your address and phone number should appear in the lower left or right corner. Once your script has found an agent, then the agent's name will appear on the title page. Your agent will be able to show you how to do that.

If you register your script with the Writers Guild or other service, you do not need to indicate as much on the title page. Although you want to register your script, posting the notice is neither necessary nor recommended. In other words, all you need is the title, author, and point of contact. That's it. (For information on the Writers Guild and other registration services, see Books IV and V, or the index.)

TYPEFACE, MARGINS, AND TABS

Typeface

Always use a font or typeface that is 10-pitch, such as Courier and PICA. Do not use a proportional font, such as what is commonly used in typesetting. It compresses letters and characters to get more words on a line. All books and magazines use a proportional font. The letters are squeezed together. The right margin is justified. It looks great, but it's anathema for screenplays.

Here's what is wanted: A good, old-fashioned PICA or Courier 12-point, 10-pitch font with a ragged right margin. What is *point size*? This is how tall the letter or character is. What is *pitch*? Pitch refers to the number of characters that fill an inch. In other words, if you were to type ten characters side by side, print, and then measure them on the printed page, they should come to an inch. Let's try and see.

1234567890 — This is a Sabon 12-point proportional font. Ten characters measure less than an inch.

```
1234567890 -- This is a Courier 12-point, 10-pitch font.  It
works.  This is what you use in a screenplay.  It looks like
it's typed using a typewriter.
```

All of the examples in this format guidebook are in Courier so that they appear exactly the way they would appear in a script.

Why all the fuss over a font? Because the 10-pitch font is easier on the eyes of industry people who read dozens of scripts every week. It also retains the "one page equals one minute screen time" industry standard.

Margins

Because scripts are three-hole punched, the left margin should be 1.5 inches, the right margin a half inch. The top and bottom margins should be one inch each. Assuming the standard ten characters per inch (10-pitch font), that would mean a left margin at 15 (1.5 inches from the left edge of the paper) and a right margin of 80 (eight inches from the left edge of the paper). The right margin should be *ragged*.

Tabs

Although variations abound, let these standards guide you in setting your tabs:

- Left margin at 15 spaces (1.5 inches) from the left edge of the page.
- Dialogue at 25 spaces (2.5 inches); that's 10 spaces from the *left margin*.
- Actor's instructions at 31 (3.1 inches); that's 16 spaces from the *left margin*.
- Character's name at 37 (3.7 inches); that's 22 spaces from the *left margin*.

Make sure your dialogue does not extend beyond 60 spaces (6.0 inches) from the left edge of the page (in other words, a line of dialogue should be no wider than 3.5 inches), and actor's instructions beyond 50 spaces. The above guides are not written in stone—some writers indent 12 for dialogue, some indent 7 for actor's instructions, etc. As mentioned, a ragged right margin is preferred to a justified right margin.

PAGE NUMBERS

Page numbers should appear in the upper right, flush right, after which you double-space and resume your writing. Your first page does not carry a page number. (To those using typewriters instead of computers: If, in your final draft, you double the length of an early scene—say, on page 70—and you don't want to retype all the page numbers on the subsequent pages of the script, consider numbering the "extra" page *70A*. Anyone having a script that is overlong may consider using this trick as well.)

[A] THE FIRST PAGE

Some writers write their title, CAPPED and underscored, at the top of the first page; but the great majority don't. A screenplay begins with FADE IN, as demonstrated on page 63. The example below is also correct, but includes a master scene heading.

```
FADE IN:

EXT. LARGE UNIVERSITY CAMPUS - DAY

Walkways are jammed with students.
```

Credits

Don't worry about where to place your opening and closing CREDITS. They're *not* required for the spec script. Besides, it's very hard to judge just how long it will take the credits to roll. If you insist on indicating the credits because you have this neat little opening written, then use this format:

```
ROLL CREDITS.   Or . . .   BEGIN CREDITS.
```

And after the last opening credit . . .

```
END CREDITS.
```

In the above example, CREDITS is treated as a "heading." However, it can also be included in the body of the description. The word TITLES is often used in place of CREDITS. Again, I advise against indicating CREDITS or TITLES.

The End

At the end of your screenplay, double-space (or triple or quadruple), type *The End*, and center it. As an alternative, double-space, flush right, and type FADE OUT.

Headings

Screenplays and teleplays consist of three parts: 1) Headings (sometimes called *slug lines*), 2) Description, and 3) Dialogue. This section deals with headings. Headings always appear in CAPS and come in two general categories: Master scene headings and secondary headings.

[B] MASTER SCENE HEADINGS

A master scene heading consists of three parts.

First is the location of the camera. If the camera is located outside or outdoors, then use EXT. for EXTERIOR. If it is indoors, then use INT. for INTERIOR. (See page 77 for a discussion of "Camera Placement.")

Occasionally, the action moves back and forth through a doorway or opening. This can create a large number of master scene headings. Sometimes a scene begins outside, but quickly moves inside (or vice versa). In such cases, the following heading is permissible:

INT./EXT. CLASSROOM - DAY.

The **second** part of a master scene heading is the location of the scene, the place where everything is happening. Usually one or two words will suffice. At code [C] on page 63, the location is a small classroom. I use the word "small" only because I don't want the director using one of those large, semi-circular auditoriums. I want a more intimate scene and perhaps a modest budget. Generally, you want master scene headings to be short and specific.

The **third** part of the master scene heading is the time of day. Most often this will be DAY or NIGHT. Avoid terms like DUSK, DAWN, LATE AFTERNOON, EARLY EVENING, HIGH NOON, GLOAMING, or the time on the clock. Use these only if absolutely necessary.

Occasionally, SAME is used to indicate that the scene takes place at the same time as, or just after, the previous scene. Sometimes LATER is used to indicate passage of time.

```
INT. KITCHEN - SAME
```

If a scene requires further identification because it is a dream, for example, such a clarification may be added as a **fourth** part of the master scene heading. Suppose your screenplay jumps all over time. In that case, you could additionally indicate the date (or the season) of the scene. Here are two examples:

```
EXT. TOKYO BAY - TWILIGHT - SUMMER, 1945

INT. BEDROOM - NIGHT - MARTY'S DREAM
```

Technically, if any of the three (or four) elements of a master scene heading change, you have a new scene, and must type in a new master scene heading with the change. Headings never appear as the last item on the page.

There are many ways to express a master scene heading. Here are the most common.

```
INT. CLASSROOM - DAY
INT.  CLASSROOM - DAY
```

As usual, variations abound, but the general form remains the same.

Recently, I have seen some scripts with master scenes bolded. I suspect this might become common practice in years to come, but until it does, I wouldn't bold anything.

[C] SPACING BETWEEN SCENES

Do you space twice or three times between master scenes? The correct answer is three, but twice is acceptable. In fact, most scripts double-space. One rule of thumb: If your screenplay is running too long, double-space; if it is running short, triple-space.

Do not number your scenes (or shots) in a spec script. This is done by a production person after the final draft is sold and the script has gone into production.

SECONDARY HEADINGS

Master scenes often contain more than one dramatic unit, each of which requires a heading. These can be individual SHOTS (although you will seldom, if ever, use the term SHOT), or side locations, or specific instances that require highlighting. They provide you with ways to break up master scenes. Most of the rules regarding master scene headings apply to these as well.

Headings are always in CAPS and never appear as the last item on a page. Although you may triple-space between master scenes, you normally double-space before or after secondary headings. Here are the most common uses of secondary headings. Let's start with an example.

In CASABLANCA, much of the action takes place at Rick's Cafe. These scenes can be quite long unless they are broken up into smaller scenes. For example, the master scene would be:

```
INT. RICK'S PLACE - NIGHT
```

A few paragraphs into the scene and we go to a specific spot at Rick's place.

```
AT THE BAR
```

or

```
IN THE GAMING ROOM
```

We are still at Rick's Cafe. If we cut to the same location, but time has passed, we normally have a new master scene, and write:

```
INT. RICK'S PLACE - LATER
```

But we can probably get away with just:

```
LATER
```

Another advantage of using secondary headings is you can direct the camera without using camera terms.

Suppose you want to focus on characters in an intense scene. Instead of the common ANGLE ON ILSA or CLOSE ON ILSA, you simply write:

```
     ILSA

     removes a gun from her purse and points it at Rick.

     RICK

     stops cold in his tracks.  Looks at her in surprise.
```

Now you are using character names as headings, and the story flows easily without being encumbered by camera directions. Here is an excerpt from my screenplay, A WINDOW IN TIME. Note how this directs the camera without using technical terms.

```
     Abu nods gratefully to the Man in Khakis, then rushes to

     THE TEMPLE BASE

     where a small hole has been cut into the foundation.  The
     Man in Khakis leads Abu into the blackness.

     INSIDE THE CATACOMBS

     Abu and the Man in Khakis crawl on all fours toward the
     torch light ahead, and finally into

     A LARGE CIRCULAR CHAMBER

     where torches illuminate the stoic faces of a dozen workers
     standing back against the single, circular wall.
```

You may have noticed in the above example that I get away without using master scene headings where they would normally be required. It is clear that the catacombs are an INTERIOR and that it's still DAY, and the same is true of the circular chamber. Be careful, however, not to get too creative. You never want to lose or confuse a reader.

Other common secondary headings are the MONTAGE, the SERIES OF SHOTS, the INSERT, and the INTERCUT.

[D] MONTAGE and SERIES OF SHOTS

If I didn't use the MONTAGE sequence on page 64, I would need more master scene headings than Carter has pills. A MONTAGE is a sequence of brief shots expressing the same or similar idea, such as a passage of time, or a stream of consciousness. Here's an alternate format for the MONTAGE.

```
MONTAGE - SUZY AND BILL HAVE FUN TOGETHER

-- They run along the beach.  Suzy raises her countenance
   against the ocean spray.

-- They bicycle through a park.

-- Bill buys Suzy ice cream at a small stand. She stuffs it
   into his face.  The patrons chuckle.
```

And, of course you would end the montage with BACK TO SCENE or END MON-TAGE or new Master Scene Heading. It's okay to include dialogue in a MONTAGE sequence, but generally the focus is on bits of action.

Similar to the MONTAGE is the SERIES OF SHOTS, consisting of quick shots that tell a story. They lead to some dramatic resolution or dramatic action, whereas a MONTAGE focuses on a single concept (in the professor's case, hysteria or irrational fear). Here's an example of how to format the SERIES OF SHOTS.

```
SERIES OF SHOTS

A)  The classroom spins.

B)  The professor, in a panic, jabs the computer tab key.

C)  He tosses the computer out the window.

D)  He peers out the window, clutching his little dog.

E)  Dean Zelda Zack rides up on her swagger stick, hurls the
    computer back at him, and CACKLES.

BACK TO SCENE
```

The MONTAGE is used more than the SERIES OF SHOTS. Even when the sequence is a true SERIES OF SHOTS, the MONTAGE format is often used. Sometimes the heading MONTAGE is used and then the shots are numbered exactly like the SERIES OF SHOTS example above. The rules are very fluid here. Use these devices sparingly.

Generally, a MONTAGE in the script is scored to music in the movie. For example, the above MONTAGE of Suzy and Bill could be lengthened to be accompanied by a love song—the MONTAGE concept would be "falling in love." The training MONTAGE from ROCKY is another example. Thus, the word MONTAGE usually means: *Put the hit song here.* Now, don't *you* indicate the musical selection you'd prefer. In fact, don't refer to music at all. That's someone else's job. (For more on music, see page 85.)

FLASHBACKS

Since the FLASHBACK is often abused by beginning writers, make sure that your use of it pays off dramatically. In terms of formatting, handle a FLASHBACK like a MONTAGE. (Note that secondary headings are often followed by a space-hypen-space and then an explanation of the heading, as with the example below.)

```
FLASHBACK - THE PROFESSOR'S BEDROOM BACK HOME
```

```
A much younger professor, in a panic, jabs the tab key of
the computer.  In frustration, he hurls the computer out
the window.  He peers out, then clutches his little dog as
a young Zelda Zack rides up to the window on a broom.  She
CACKLES and rides off.
```

```
BACK TO PRESENT DAY
```

Another way to handle the above is to write the master scene heading as follows:

```
INT. THE BEDROOM BACK HOME - DAY - FLASHBACK
```

If a FLASHBACK covers several scenes, then indicate it with FLASHBACK SEQUENCE. Once the FLASHBACK SEQUENCE is over, indicate PRESENT DAY at the end of the next master scene heading, or simply write:

```
BACK TO PRESENT DAY
```

A FLASHBACK is written in present tense.

[E] INSERT

The INSERT (also known as the CUTAWAY) is used to bring something small into full frame. This can be a book, news headline, sign, contract, letter, or a leather pouch filled with mints. You use the INSERT because it is important to draw special attention to the item. In the case of a letter or a document with a lot of text, you may wish to use the INSERT as follows.

```
INT. LIMO - LATE NIGHT
```

```
As Silvester steps into the limo, the chauffeur hands him a
letter and bats his eyes like an ostrich.
```

```
                    CHAUFFEUR
         Your wife, sir.

Silvester tears the letter open as the door SLAMS shut.

INSERT - THE LETTER

         "Dearest Darling Silvester,

         I am leaving for Loon City to start
         a turkey ranch.  Don't try to follow,
         my peacock, or I'll have your cockatoo
         strangled.  There's plenty of chicken
         in the refrigerator.  I love you, you
         goosey duck.

                    Your ex-chick, Birdie"

BACK TO SCENE

Silvester smiles like the cat who ate the canary.

                    SILVESTER
         So long, Tweetie Pie.
```

Once you have written the INSERT, it is good manners to bring us BACK TO SCENE (See Code [E] on page 65), although this can also be done with a new master scene heading or secondary heading. In any situation like this, opt for clarity and a smooth flow of the story.

INTERCUT

A full explanation of this secondary heading plus examples can be found under "Telephone Conversations" on page 90.

[F] ESTABLISHING SHOT

At the beginning of a movie or scene, there is often an establishing shot to give us an idea of where on earth we are. Don't use the camera direction ESTABLISHING SHOT; simply describe the image. In my script, we are in a university campus classroom. Note that paragraph code [F] in the script example on page 63 goes from general to specific, from long shots down to a close shot.

Here are two ways to present an establishing shot.

EXT. NEW YORK CITY - DAY - ESTABLISHING

or

EXT. NEW YORK CITY - DAY

Manhattan sparkles in the sunlight.

The second example is preferred because it is more interesting, plus it directs the camera without using camera directions. It's obviously a long shot of the entire city.

[G]   CAMERA PLACEMENT

In the scene beginning at reference code [B] on page 63, the camera is inside the classroom. We know this because the master scene heading is INT. SMALL CLASSROOM - DAY. The INT. means the camera is inside the classroom. However, the camera can SEE (at the first reference code [G]) out through the window to the young woman in pigtails and a pinafore.

Likewise, in the next scene, the camera is outside the classroom (by virtue of the EXT.) "looking" into the classroom as the professor performs cartwheels down the aisle (at the second reference code [G]). Thus, the window is used as a transitional device between scenes. (See page 70 for information on master scene headings and page 83 for information on directing the camera.)

[H]   The master scene heading is EXT. CLASSROOM - DAY. It could as easily have been EXT. PHONE BOOTH - DAY. The reason it isn't is that I felt the relationship between the phone booth and classroom would not be quite as clear. The choice, as always, is yours. Always strive to write clearly so that the reader can easily visualize the images and actions of your scene.

Description

Screenplays and teleplays consist of three parts: 1) Headings, 2) Description, and 3) Dialogue. We will now discuss description.

Narrative description is written in present tense because we view a film in present time. Double-space between paragraphs and do not indent. Keep your narrative description (and dialogue) on the lean side, providing only what is absolutely necessary to progress the story while emphasizing important actions and moments. Try to keep your paragraphs to four lines (not four sentences) or less, five lines max.

Beginning at [B] on page 63, there are a few things that I feel are necessary to set up for the sequence to work. First, my professor "looks" different from the stereotypical professor; plus, I establish that this scene is about formatting. Also, the professor has a leather pouch filled with candy mints. The pouch of mints is of tremendous importance to the story, so I take two lines to describe it.

I could have chosen to give the pouch a separate paragraph to give it more emphasis and to imply that the pouch deserves a separate camera shot.

Please notice that I do not describe anything in this classroom or even how the professor dresses. In this scene, I don't need to. Generally, physical descriptions of locations and characters should be sparse. (Please see "Character Descriptions" on page 79.)

In addition, don't write anything that can't actually be represented on the screen. Thoughts, feelings, motives, recollections, and writer's explanations of what's going on must be expressed in terms of action or dialogue, with action often being the better choice of the two.

Important action segments that may take a lot of screen time can be stretched out on the page by using short paragraphs and emphasizing specific images and emotions.

Duke sneers at the catcher. Taps the bat twice on the
plate and spits. A brown wad splatters on the plate.

The catcher refuses to notice. Keeps his eyes ahead.

Smiley steps off the rubber. Nervously works the rosin
bag. Wipes the sweat from his forehead with his arm.

Duke leans over the plate like he owns it. Allows himself
a self-satisfied grin.

And so on.

[I] CHARACTER FIRST APPEARANCES

The name PROFESSOR (top of page 63) is in CAPS because this is his first appearance in the screenplay. CHARLIE is likewise capitalized because it's the first time he appears in the story. So why wasn't "twenty students" capitalized? Because they weren't important enough to warrant drawing the reader's focus to them. You do not need to capitalize the names of characters who do not have speaking parts, but it is not incorrect if you do. (Please see page 80 for "Characters With More Than One Name.")

When a name in CAPS is followed by a possessive, the *s* is placed in lower case:

A BANSHEE's scream shatters the silence.

CHARACTER DESCRIPTIONS

When a character first appears in the script, you have an opportunity to suggest something of his/her nature. In most cases we do not need to know the character's height, weight, hair color, or the fact that she looks exactly like Cher. Do not give a driver's license description of your character and do not pin the name of a famous actor or actress on your character because it limits who can star in your screenplay. Here is how my co-writer and I describe our lead in TABLOID:

JAKE BURNS sports a week's growth and unruly hair. Everything about him, from his wrinkled suit to his careless
manner, suggests he doesn't give a damn about anything. In
fact, Jake would pass as a bum if it weren't for that hard,
confident look in his eye that tells you he's a man to be
dealt with.

Yes, we take certain liberties here, but so can you. This is one of the few places where you can. Notice that Jake not only has certain clothes, but he carries an attitude. He's been somewhere before he got here—he's a human with emotions and a past. Here are descriptions of two minor characters in my screenplay A WINDOW IN TIME:

```
J. C. WARDLE, a sexless woman with an ambitious stride,
snatches a paper from the hand of PALMER, her male aide,
who looks more like a big geek with a notebook than the
Defense Department agent that he is.
```

Like Jake Burns in TABLOID, Wardle has an attitude. And Palmer has a prop that he'll be identified with throughout the script. In BODY HEAT, the central character is introduced as follows:

```
...we see the naked back and head of NED RACINE.
```

In the subsequent paragraph, we learn he that Ned is wearing shorts, smoking a cigarette, and gazing at a distant fire. That's it.

[J] CHARACTERS WITH MORE THAN ONE NAME

CALCUTTA COTTER is in CAPS because although she was first introduced as a YOUNG WOMAN (below [M] on page 63), we are now learning her name for the first time. (See page 79 for more on "Character First Appearances.") If a character has more than one name that is used in the screenplay, you must take pains not to confuse the reader. You may give the character as many names, nicknames, or descriptions (the professor, the teacher, the great communicator, etc.) as you wish in the *description* section of the screenplay. But the character must be *referred* to by the same name in the dialogue caption (I'm not referring to the actual words of the dialogue, but to the character's name that appears in CAPS above the dialogue—that name should be the same throughout the script, with rare exception). (Also see "Character Cue" on page 87.)

VISUAL CHARACTERIZATION

This is a good place to mention that movies are visual, so it doesn't hurt to give your character a visual identification such as Charlie's peanut butter and flies.

Toward the bottom of page 63, Dean Zelda Zack, like the other characters, is described in sparse terms. However, I give her three things that add to her character *visually*: a swagger stick, a metal sign, and a polished desk.

Also on page 63, I give the classroom its only physical description, and that is the fact that there is a window where Charlie sits. This is mentioned only because of its importance later as a transitional element. (See page 82 for more on transitions, and page 79, "Character Descriptions," for examples of visual characterizations.)

ACTION VERBS

Because a screenplay is written in present tense, it's easy to find yourself writing like this: John *is looking* at Mary. Suzy *is walking* past the cafe. Replace those progressive forms with simple present tense: John *looks* at Mary. Suzy *walks* past the cafe.

Now go one step further and create something even more active and concrete: John *gawks* at Mary, or John *gazes* at Mary. Suzy *scampers* down the sidewalk, or Suzy *sashays* down the sidewalk. Now the reader can more easily visualize the action and gain a greater sense of the character as well. And without a single adverb.

Concrete, specific nouns also help us "see." *Dinghy, rowboat, yacht,* and *pontoon* are more descriptive than *boat.* And no adjectives are needed.

[K] SIGNS, NEWS HEADLINES, SONGS, BOOKS, MAGAZINES, NOTES, AND LETTERS

There are many ways to handle signs. I chose to put CINEMA DEPARTMENT in CAPS, which is generally preferred. I could have as easily put it in quotes (like I did at code [K] on page 63), or underscored it, or any combination. Never use italics, however, to set apart anything. Stay with one font throughout.

News headlines, name plates, song titles, book titles, names of magazines, plaques, signs on doors, etc., are usually placed in CAPS. Sometimes the contents of notes, letters, or documents need to be shown. Here, you may want to use the INSERT. The INSERT is explained on pages 75-76.

[L] SOUNDS

The general rule of thumb is to place important sounds in CAPS. This is why I capitalized BUZZING (on page 63). Do not use the archaic: SFX. BUZZING FLIES.

[M] SPECIAL EFFECTS

The climax of this little scene (code [M] on page 63) is Charlie catching a mint on his nose and barking like a seal. This may require a special effect. In the past, this may have been written FX. CHARLIE CATCHING A MINT ON HIS NOSE, but not now. (By the way, FX. and SPFX. both mean Special Effects; and SFX. means Sound Effects.) There is another possible special effect at [M] on page 64.

Don't use FX. or SPFX. unless it's absolutely necessary for the clarity of the story. Since special effects are costly, you don't need to advertise to the studio or producer how expensive your movie is going to be. Sell the script first. After the script is sold, a production person will go through your script and identify all the special effects.

SUBTITLES AND SUPERS

Subtitles are words that are superimposed on the screen to add some special meaning to what we're seeing and/or hearing.

EXT. CASTLE ON A LAKE - DAY

```
A beautiful storybook castle.  SUPER the legend:  "Once
upon a time there lived a princess...."
```

Or...

```
A beautiful storybook castle.  The words "Once upon a time
there lived a princess" FILTER INTO VIEW.
```

Or, you could simply write SUBTITLE: or SUPER: as its own heading and give it a paragraph of its own. Subtitles and superimpositions are capitalized because they are special effects. (For information on dialogue subtitles, see page 89.)

[N] TRANSITIONS

The SLAMMING of telephone receivers (bottom of page 63 and top of page 64) is a transitional ploy. I am suggesting to the director that once Calcutta SLAMS her phone, that we should CUT immediately to the professor SLAMMING his phone. This situation could also be handled with the MATCH CUT, discussed next.

EDITING DIRECTIONS

If I wrote the transition described above to include the editing direction MATCH CUT, I would have written it as follows:

The dean CHORTLES. Calcutta smiles, then SLAMS the receiver.

MATCH CUT:

INT. CLASSROOM - DAY

The professor SLAMS the phone receiver.

The MATCH CUT is used to match an object or image from one scene to the next. The above transition of Calcutta slamming her phone receiver to the professor slamming his is an example. However, an editing direction may not be necessary here because the transition is obvious. Use the MATCH CUT when the *match* is not already obvious.

The use of CUT TO is usually unnecessary. Obviously, one must CUT at the end of a scene, so why indicate it? Nevertheless, it is correct, but use it sparingly. If such editing tools as the WIPE, IRIS, FLIP, and DISSOLVE are important to the story, then include them in the script, but be judicious. My advice is to avoid them. Stay with occasional uses of CUT TO and MATCH CUT.

CAMERA DIRECTIONS

Let's break current convention and rewrite this section utilizing our vast arsenal of camera and editing directions. Note as you read the bad example below how the technical directions detract from the story and slow down the read for the reader. (By the way, CU means CLOSE UP, and ECU means EXTREME CLOSE UP.)

INT. CLASSROOM - NEAR SUNSET

CU PROFESSOR SLAMMING the receiver of his toy phone.

PULL BACK and BOOM to ESTABLISH classroom.

PROFESSOR'S POV: CAMERA PANS the class.

DISSOLVE TO:

LOW ANGLE of the professor -- confident.

```
WIDE ANGLE of THE STUDENTS as they SIMMER with interest.

ZIP ZOOM TO ECU doorknob opening.   PULL BACK TO REVEAL
Calcutta coming through the door.   DOLLY WITH Calcutta's
SHUFFLING feet as she makes her way to her desk.

CLOSE ON the professor expounding.

SWIRLING SHOT of the professor in increasingly larger con-
centric circles.
```

Please, I beg you, don't do this to your script! First, you may insult the director. Second, it breaks up the narrative flow, and makes the script harder to read. Third, you take the chance of showing off your ignorance. Fourth, readers are not pleased. So, go easy. Remember, the story's the thing. Concentrate on that. It's true that most shooting scripts (the scripts you buy to read) contain many such camera directions and technical devices. Keep in mind that these directions and devices were likely added *after* the script was sold to prepare it for the shoot.

There is a secret way to indicate all the camera directions your heart desires without using the technical terms. Simply be creative and write the script so that they're implied. On page 64, I write:

```
When she speaks again, her lips are not unlike those of
Orson Welles when he said, "Rosebud."
```

This may not be especially creative, but it is a very definite ECU (Extreme Close Up). At [N] on page 64, I use the word "hand" to imply a CLOSE UP or ANGLE of the phone SLAMMING. His "surveying" might imply a POV (Point of View) shot, but certainly it is a MEDIUM SHOT of some kind. The students SIMMERING with interest is a REACTION SHOT of the entire class or REACTION SHOTS of individual students. (See how I give the director a choice!) If it's tremendously important to the scene that Charlie react strongly, I will write in a separate paragraph:

```
Charlie is so excited that he leaps from his seat and ex-
ecutes a flawless back flip.
```

Although correct, avoid headings like: ANGLE ON CHARLIE, CLOSE ON CHARLIE, and ANOTHER ANGLE. Noting the examples on pages 72-73, you may decide to write:

```
CHARLIE

leaps from his seat and executes a flawless back flip.
```

The *spec* script's emphasis is on lean, visual writing. Your goal is to create images while avoiding the use of technical terms. Instead of CLOSE UP OF DARLENE'S TEAR, you write *A tear rolls down Darlene's cheek.* (It's obviously a close up.)

Instead of JAKE'S POV - The killer advances toward him, you write *Jake freezes as he watches the killer advance toward him.* You're still directing the camera, even though you're not using camera directions. In RAIDERS OF THE LOST ARK, *What he sees:* is used in lieu of the POV. (Also see Code [O] below.)

In conclusion, use camera directions and editing directions sparingly, only when they are really needed to clarify the action or add significantly to the story's impact.

[O] POV
The heading at Code [D] on page 64 could have been written: THE PROFESSOR'S POV. And that would be correct. Instead, I avoided the inclusion of a camera direction, but still made it clear (at Code [O]) that the spinning room is seen from the professor's point of view (POV). For another example of POV, see above (JAKE'S POV).

WE SEE and TO REVEAL
Writers often use the camera direction WE SEE. Another favorite is PULL BACK TO REVEAL or REVEALING. Although correct, they are seldom the most interesting way to convey the action and details of the scene to your reader.

B.g. and f.g.
B.g. stands for *background* and f.g. stands for *foreground*. These terms may be used in your narrative description to clarify action (for example: the T-Rex moves in the b.g.), but I recommend you use them sparingly. If you must use them, just write out the word (the T-Rex moves in the background).

MUSIC

Don't indicate music in your script unless it is essential to the progression of your story. If music is an integral part of your story—a movie about a rock singer, for example—then you may wish to indicate music in a general way:

A HEAVY METAL RIFF rips through the silence.

Or . . .

Upbeat ROCK MUSIC plays.

Another way to indicate music generically is to describe the sound of it: The radio BLASTS. Keep in mind that since music is a SOUND, you usually emphasize it by placing it in CAPS.

Any of the above choices, however, are risky. A more professional approach is to intimate music indirectly by suggesting an emotional mood. You'll manage this through description, dialogue, and character. The director and composer will pick up on your *vibe*, and select or compose music that matches the emotion of the scene.

Regardless of whether you indicate music or not, the one thing you should *not* do is pick specific songs. Unless you own the rights to the songs, you are creating a no-win situation for yourself and a legal hurdle for anyone interested in buying the script.

[P] AUTHOR'S INTRUSION

In virtually every literary form, author's intrusion is unacceptable. In a screenplay, it is permissible if it helps tell the story or clarifies something. However, don't overdo it and don't get too cute. Don't interrupt the narrative flow of the story. When in doubt, stay out. At code [P] on page 65, I intrude with my sentence, "Can he do it?"

[Q] CONTINUED

If a scene does not conclude at the bottom of any page, it has been customary in the past to double-space and type (CONTINUED) at the lower right (flushed right); and type CONTINUED: at the upper left (flushed left) of the next page, followed by two vertical spaces, after which the writing resumes. This is no longer done.

SPECIAL NOTES

Once every blue moon you get a creative idea that does not fit any known formatting guidelines. In these few cases, simply write a note in a separate paragraph. You may place the note in parenthesis if you'd like, although it's not necessary. Here's an example from one of my old scripts:

```
(NOTE:  This scene is SHOT in BLACK AND WHITE.  It should
appear old and scratched as if it originated from a 1950's
public information library.  There are intentional JUMP
CUTS.)
```

Dialogue

Screenplays and teleplays consist of three parts: 1) Headings, 2) Description, and 3) Dialogue. This section deals with dialogue.

The dialogue sections of a screenplay consist of three parts.

[R] CHARACTER CAPTION

First is the character name or caption, sometimes called the *character cue*. It always appears in CAPS. A character is referred to by exactly the same name throughout the screenplay. In the narrative description, you may use a variety names, but the character cue for a character should be the same throughout the script. (See page 80.)

ACTOR'S DIRECTION

Directly below the character name is the actor's instructions, sometimes called *personal direction* or *parentheticals* or *wrylies*. These can provide useful and helpful tips, usually suggesting the subtext, or attitude of the character. However, keep in mind that they are optional and should be used with moderation. (See example on page 65.) Don't use them to describe actions, unless those actions can be described in two or three words, such as "tipping his hat." (See example near code [W] on page 64.)

CHARACTER'S SPEECH

The third part of dialogue is the speech itself, the words to be spoken. Because speech is indented, you do not use quotation marks or italics to indicate the spoken word. Avoid hyphenation and maintain a ragged right margin. Each speech should be as brief as possible, and generally convey one thought. One or two sentences is plenty in most cases. Fragments are welcome. Avoid long speeches. Don't overuse exclamation points. Avoid underlining words for emphasis unless it is crucial to understand the story. When working with dialects and accents, sprinkle in bits of dialect and phonetically spelled words just to give us a flavor of the accent or regional influence. Make sure the speeches are easy to read. For information on dialogue punctuation, see page 92. For information on where to set your tabs, see page 68.

[S] CONTINUING AND CONT'D

On page 64, Calcutta says, "I wanna know something." The class hushes. Then, at [S], she *continues* her speech. In the past, this would have been handled in one of two ways:

```
                    CALCUTTA
                  (continuing)
        The tabs.  Where do I set them?


                    CALCUTTA (cont'd)
        The tabs.  Where do I set them?
```

This device, however, has almost completely fallen out of use.

MORE

When someone's dialogue does not conclude at the bottom of the page, type (MORE) directly below the last line of dialogue.

```
                      BUGSY
        I am at the bottom of the page,
        running out of room, and would...
                      (MORE)
```

```
At the top of the next page, continue as follows:
```

```
                      BUGSY (cont'd)
        ...like to continue my speech.
```

A better alternative might be to simply conclude the speech at the bottom of the page or move it all to the top of the next page. You can cheat occasionally on your top and bottom margins (not on your left and right margins).

An equally correct alternative to (cont'd) is (CONT'D).

[T] OFF SCREEN (OS) and VOICE OVER (VO)

OFF SCREEN, at code [T] on page 65, indicates that Charlie is in the scene—he's at the location of the scene—but that he is not in the camera frame. We hear his voice, but do not see him on the screen. Why do I want Charlie OFF SCREEN? Because I want the camera to focus on the professor, whose back is now to the class. Now, if Charlie is not only off screen but also out of the scene (not in the classroom), and the professor HEARS his voice—say, in his mind—then this is a VOICE OVER as follows:

```
                    CHARLIE (VO)
             You're done for, old man.
```

The voice trails off. The professor sees no one.

If Charlie is in the scene and hears his own voice in his head, that's still VOICE OVER.

Narration is VOICE OVER. In cases where a character is on screen and we hear his thoughts or he narrates his own story, use the VOICE OVER. In phone conversations where the person on the other line is not "in the scene" but we hear the voice, this would be a VOICE OVER. (See "Telephone Voice" on page 90.) Recently, I've seen scripts where VO is not used in telephone conversations, and that's okay as long as the script is clear and not confusing. (Note: Some writers write O.S. and V.O.)

OVERLAPPING DIALOGUE

There are two ways to handle overlapping and simultaneous dialogue. One is to simply indicate "overlapping" or "simultaneous" in the parenthetical actor's instructions. A less preferred method (because it is difficult to read) is to treat the dialogue the same way you treat subtitles. An example follows.

Subtitles
Subtitles are words that are superimposed on the screen to add some special meaning to what we're seeing and/or hearing. Now here's an example of subtitles that are used to translate or otherwise comment on dialogue. This method could also be used for simultaneous dialogue. Simply place one character on the left and the other on the right.

```
INT. SPACESHIP CONTROL ROOM - NIGHT

Diptar enters the large room and bows before Grand Master.

        GRAND MASTER              SUBTITLES
   Raltar!                    Report!

          DIPTAR                  SUBTITLES
   Orf pok etar vespar.       The brain evacuator is ready.
   Nit etular orf vorpar      The earth specimens are in
   quex glipular.             place.

        GRAND MASTER              SUBTITLES
        (deeply felt)         Soon we will have complete
   Flippar eglip xerox        command of their language,
   clinggu, kalipsu...        customs, and...
   zzzzzzzipar!               reproductive techniques!
```

No doubt, you recognize this scene from my classic script RATMAN FROM SATURN.

[U] THE TELEPHONE VOICE

Voices coming through telephones, walkie-talkies, radios, and similar devices are VOICE OVERS. Sometimes I see: *(on phone)* or *(amplified)* or the antiquated *(filtered)* typed adjacent to the name. In any case, the person speaking is obviously not in camera and not at the scene location. At code [U] on page 63, I use *(on phone)* for clarity; normally, I'd use *(VO)*. For a discussion of VOICE OVER and OFF SCREEN, see page 89.

Television
Treat the television set as a separate character. If there is a specific character who is on television, simply indicate as much in your description and type the character's name as the character caption or cue. If you want to be especially clear, add *(on TV)* as follows:

```
                    JOCK JIM (on TV)
          Hi, Mom.  We're number one!
```

[V] TELEPHONE CONVERSATIONS

There are lots of ways to handle phone conversations. At code [V] on page 63, I use the INTERCUT. This indicates to the director that I want to inter-cut (or cross-cut) between the two people who are speaking on the phone. I want to SEE both people (not at the same moment, of course). The INTERCUT example on page 63 is such a short conversation that it is really unnecessary to INTERCUT. I only did it to demonstrate its use to you.

Since the INTERCUT may also be used to present two scenes simultaneously, it can be utilized as follows:

```
INTERCUT - JOHN'S BEDROOM/MARY'S KITCHEN
```

Or, you may indicate INTERCUT, then double-space and describe the scenes of situations in the narrative description. Finally, you'll double-space and conclude with either END INTERCUT or a heading. At the bottom of page 63, my INTERCUT example ends, but I do not indicate END INTERCUT because I "cut" to a heading at the top of page 64.

The INTERCUT device gives the director complete freedom as to *when* to intercut between speakers. (He/she has complete freedom anyway, so why not be gracious?) The reason you use this device is that otherwise you would have to write a master scene heading with each change of speaker. This can become laborious and interrupt the story flow. On the other hand, it may improve the story and give you more control over whom the camera is on at any point in the conversation. Let's rewrite the scene that begins at [H] on page 63 without the INTERCUT, using master scene headings.

EXT. CLASSROOM - DAY

The woman in the phone booth is CALCUTTA COTTER. With the phone to her ear, she turns toward the classroom window and frowns at what she sees — the professor doing cartwheels down the aisle between his cheering students. She turns back to the phone.

                    DEAN ZACK (VO)
          Make him pay, Calcutta...

INT. DEAN'S OFFICE - DAY

DEAN ZELDA ZACK stands at her desk with a swagger stick tucked under her arm. A big sign that says "DEAN, CINEMA DEPARTMENT" sits on her polished desk.

                    DEAN ZACK
          ...Make him pay.

INT. PHONE BOOTH - DAY

Calcutta's excitement is subdued by doubt.

                    CALCUTTA
                 (to the phone)
          It'll work?

INT. DEAN'S OFFICE - DAY

Zack's confident smile reveals gold caps over her front teeth.

                    DEAN ZACK
          Stumps him every time.

The swagger stick slashes the desk. The delirious dean CHORTLES with satisfaction.

EXT. PHONE BOOTH - DAY

The CHORTLING can be heard through the phone receiver. Calcutta smiles, then SLAMS the receiver.

Now let's take a third tack. Suppose you don't want the camera on Dean Zelda Zack, nor do you want to hear the dear dean. In such a situation, the conversation would read something like this:

```
EXT. CLASSROOM - DAY

With the phone to her ear, CALCUTTA COTTER turns toward the
classroom window and frowns at what she sees — the profes-
sor doing cartwheels down the aisle between his cheering
students.  She turns abruptly to the phone.

                    CALCUTTA
          I'll make him pay, all right --
                    (pause)
          You're sure it'll work?
                    (nodding)
          Beautiful.

Calcutta urges a smile, then SLAMS the receiver.
```

This version also works well. The only thing we're missing is the identity of Calcutta's information source. It may serve the script better dramatically to withhold the name of this person. Ask yourself: What is the best way to move the story forward?

[W] DIALOGUE PUNCTUATION

The use of the dash (--) and the ellipsis (...) has become very clouded in recent years. Usually, they are used to make dialogue look like...well -- er, dialogue.

There used to be very definite literary rules about these. Today they are used interchangeably and you may use them anyway you like—whatever feels good to you to make your dialogue look conversational. (Be careful not to overuse them.) However, understanding their actual use in terms of writing dialogue can be very helpful in presenting a consistent pattern in your written communication.

-- The dash indicates a sudden shift or break in thought, or to show emphasis. It is used when one character interrupts another, or shifts his thought, or a character is interrupted by a sound or an action, or a character speaks as if interrupted or with sudden emphasis.

The dash is written two different ways:

Example 1 -- This is the example for narrative
              description and dialogue.

Example 2 -   This is the example for headings.

... The ellipsis is used for continuity. A character will start speaking, then pause, and then continue. When a character is interrupted, and then continues later, the ellipsis is used instead of the dash.

Here's an example of both the dash and the ellipsis. (Also note how the dialogue is broken up with small, but important, actions.)

EXT. BALCONY - EVENING

Coquette dabs her eyes with a handkerchief. Suddenly, Vivi blunders through the French doors. Coquette turns expect-antly, then puts on an angry face.

                    COQUETTE
          Why did you come here?

                    VIVI
          I came here to --

                    COQUETTE
          I don't want to know why you came
          here...

He moves earnestly toward her. She softens.

                    COQUETTE
          So why...
                    (raising her lips)
          ...did you...come here?

Vivi removes his hat of many feathers. His lips are now just a silly millimeter from hers. She puckers.

                    VIVI
          I came here to...

His gaze fades into a blank stare, then stupefaction.

                    COQUETTE
          You have forgotten --

                    VIVI
                    (recovering)
          But one kiss and I will remember
          why I came here.

He lays one on her, then looks joyously into her confused face.

                    VIVI
          I came here...to kiss my
          Coquette -- you!

How to format a teleplay

This section builds on information in the previous sections of this book. Sample scenes of a sitcom spec script can be found on pages 98-99.

TV Movies

A teleplay for a TV movie (called *long form* or *MOW* for "Movie-of-the-Week") is normally seven acts and about 105 pages. If you're writing such a teleplay, I recommend you use standard screenplay format. That way, you can avoid the pain of delineating acts and pacing the story's major turning points for commercial breaks. Besides, your MOW could be a feature movie. Just write it like a feature screenplay. Once your teleplay is sold, then you can convert it into the standard seven-act form.

Pilots

It is nearly impossible for novices to break into television with a new series pilot or mini-series. If you have a hot idea that you believe in, write the pilot as a TV movie (using standard screenplay format) and market it as a feature script or TV movie. That way, it will be easier to get it read. If it truly is a great series idea, the agent or producer reading it will see that potential.

Dramatic Series

If you want to write an episode for a dramatic series (usually an hour in length), then you will still use standard screenplay form. However, you will need to designate the four (or five) acts, the teaser, and tag (or epilogue). You will not indicate scenes, but you will indicate each act. You do this by writing ACT ONE or ACT 1 at the top of the page—centered and in CAPS—then double-spacing and proceeding with the first master scene heading. It's always a good idea to buy or secure a script from the series itself, since each show tends to have little formatting variations that you may want to be aware of. Contact the series producer or the script sources listed on pages 184-185. Your script will be about 54 pages, since an hour series runs about 54 minutes.

Situation Comedy
Situation comedy (sitcoms) utilizes a mutant variation of screenwriting format. That's why this section's primary focus is sitcom format. If you want to write for a specific TV show, obtain a copy of one of their scripts (see pages 184-185), since each show varies in formatting style. Sitcoms are either taped or shot in film, which is another reason variations in formatting abound. A half-hour sitcom script is about 40-45 pages in length. This differs from standard screenplay form, which is about a page per minute of screen time.

TITLE PAGE

The title page for an episodic TV show, dramatic or comedic, is similar to that of a feature script, except that the title of the episode is included along with the title of the series. Here is an example for a series entitled *L.A. Script Doctors*.

L.A. SCRIPT DOCTORS

"THE PERSPICACIOUS PROFESSOR"

You can space twice or three times between the series title and the episode title.

THE CAST LIST AND SETS LIST

Although these two lists appear on shooting scripts, you will *not* include them in your spec script. They are *not* required. If you are writing a shooting script, the cast list will include any actors already assigned to the series. Usually, the characters appearing every week are listed first, followed by any guest characters. The sets are listed in three categories: exteriors, interiors, and stock shots.

ACTS AND SCENES

All teleplays have acts. Each act ends on a turning point, followed by a commercial. Act designations are usually written out in CAPS (for example, ACT ONE), but can be written in Roman numerals. At the end of the act, break with END OF ACT ONE, centered two spaces below the end of the act. Sitcoms have two acts while one-hour dramas have four. Most often, sitcoms and drama series open with a "teaser" or "hook" and conclude with a "tag" or "epilogue."

Please note the headings and all the white space on the right side of pages 98 and 99. Most television comedy is written this way. Each time there is a change in scene, you will break to the next page. (Also see "Entrances and Exits" on page 97.)

On page 99 we have a new scene. If this were a continuation of the previous scene, I would have started at the top of the page.

NUMBERING OF PAGES, ACTS, AND SCENES

Appearing below each page number is the act and scene number. Page numbers are usually followed by a period. See examples in the upper right-hand corners of pages 98 and 99.

DESCRIPTION

Narrative description always appears parenthetically and in CAPS, and is confined to the left two-thirds of the page. This is so the director, actors, and others can scribble on the right-hand side of the page.

SOUNDS

Sounds are always given a separate line and are underscored. When Dean Zack SLAPS her swagger stick across her desk (page 99), it is obviously a sound effect. Even so, it must be written out as a separate line. The exception to this is when the sound comes out of the mouth of a character, as it does at the bottom of page 99.

UNDERSCORING

Special effects, editing directions, camera directions, master scene headings, secondary headings, entrances, exits, character first appearances, sound effects, and music appear in CAPS *and* are underscored in a situation-comedy script. (See pages 98 and 99 for examples.)

ENTRANCES AND EXITS

In television comedy, there are very few changes in scenes (sometimes none). To keep the story from bogging down, mini scenes are created by the entrances and exits of characters. If two people are already in camera, and a third appears, this third person creates a brand new mini-scene. This is of such importance that all entrances and exits are underscored, as are character first appearances.

DIALOGUE

Since there is such an emphasis on the dialogue in television comedy, it is double-spaced. Actor's instructions (personal direction) are written just like description, and are used more freely than in a screenplay. Some shows allow you to place these within the dialogue block itself.

SIMPLICITY

A sitcom is simpler than a screenplay, both in structure and in content. Comparing the screenplay scene on page 63 to the sitcom scenes on pages 98-99 should prove to be very instructive. Most sitcom episodes are blocked and shot within a week. This is one reason why there are so few changes in location and virtually no tricky shots. There is more emphasis on dialogue than action.

L.A. SCRIPT DOCTORS

"The Perspicacious Professor"

ACT ONE

Scene A

FADE IN:

INT. SMALL CLASSROOM - DAY

(ABOUT 8 STUDENTS AWAIT THE PROFESSOR,
WHO ENTERS WITH EXCITEMENT. OVER HIS
SHOULDER IS A STRAP SUPPORTING A LEATHER
POUCH, THE KIND USED BY ANIMAL TRAINERS,
ONLY THIS ONE IS FILLED WITH CANDY MINTS
INSTEAD OF FISH.)

(CHARLIE RAISES HIS HAND.)

                    CHARLIE

     Hey, Mr. Professor, how you handle

     phone calls in a script?

                    PROFESSOR

(SCINTILLATING)

     A most excellent question.

(HE TOSSES THE GRATEFUL BOY A CANDY. CHARLIE
CATCHES IT IN HIS MOUTH AND SMILES BROADLY.)

Scene B

INT. THE DEAN'S OFFICE - DAY

(CALCUTTA COTTER is in conversation with
DEAN ZELDA ZACK.)

CALCUTTA

...And then the professor gives

everyone a candy--all except me.

(DEAN ZELDA ZACK SLAPS HER SWAGGER STICK
ACROSS HER DESK.)

SOUND: THE SLAP OF THE SWAGGER STICK

DEAN ZACK

Make him pay, Calcutta, make him pay.

Now do exactly what I told you. It

stumps him every time.

(CALCUTTA EXITS.)

Now, Mr. Professor, let's see you

get out of this one!

(DEAN ZACK LAUGHS INSANELY.)

Glossary of terms not discussed elsewhere

ANGLE - Directs the camera to a particular person or object. The character's name itself could be written as a heading in CAPS and serve the same purpose. Angles (or SHOTS) can be wide, low, tight, close, high, bird's eye, etc.

AD LIB - This instructs the actors to fill in the dialogue with incidental lines.

ANAMORPHIC LENS - A lens used to shoot a wide-screen film; also, to project it onto the screen.

CRANE SHOT - A moving shot from a camera on a lift.

DISSOLVE - An editing direction where one scene "melts" into another, the former fading out while the latter fades in.

DOLLY or **TRUCK** - Picture this as a camera on wheels. Variations abound: CAMERA IN, PULL BACK TO REVEAL, TRUCK WITH, CAMERA PUSHES IN, etc.

FADE OUT - The image fades to black. This editing direction appears two spaces below the last line, flush right.

FREEZE FRAME - The image freezes on the screen and becomes a still shot. Often used with END CREDITS.

MOS - Without sound. Originated with German director Eric von Stroheim, who would tell his crew, "Ve'll shoot dis mid out sound." Use this to describe action that appears without sound. Occasionally characters will speak MOS in the b.g.

O.C. - OFF CAMERA, a term now used only in television.

OVER THE SHOULDER - Shooting over someone's shoulder from behind.

PAN - A stationary camera pivots back and forth or up and down (TILT).

PINKS - From the expression *fix it in the pinks*. Revisions of shooting scripts are usually done on colored paper.

REVERSE SHOT - When we're looking over Vivi's shoulder to Coquette, then reverse to look over Coquette's shoulder to Vivi.

SHOCK CUT - A sudden cut from one scene to another. (Also SMASH CUT.)

SLOW MOTION and **SPEEDED-UP MOTION** - You know what these are.

SPLIT SCREEN - The picture is divided into two (or more) sections.

STOCK SHOT - A film sequence previously shot and stored at a film library.

SUBLIM - A shot lasting a fraction of a second.

SUPER - A superimposition—one image (usually words) overlaid on another.

WIPE - An editing direction where one image moves another out of frame.

ZIP PAN - A super-fast PAN, creating a blurred image and a sense of quick movement.

ZOOM - A stationary camera with a zoom lens enlarges or diminishes the image.

Formatting index

7 STEPS TO A STUNNING SCRIPT

BOOK III

A Workbook

About this workbook

This workbook takes you through the seven steps of the writing process. I've tried to make it simple and easy to follow.

Each step is marked with checkpoints to keep you on track. In all, there are 26 checkpoints and over 150 key questions to help you evaluate your progress. Not every question needs to be answered. Not every checkpoint needs to be reviewed in the order it's presented. These are not hard-and-fast rules, but fluid guidelines to help you craft a stunning script. In fact, many writers like to begin the process by developing their characters; if you are one of those, you may want to do Step 4 before Steps 2 and 3.

This workbook becomes a more effective tool if you've studied the primer (Book I) first and have started or have the nascent concept for a script.

Take a moment now to congratulate yourself. You are embarking on a great journey. I hope you enjoy the adventure of creating movie people and plotting the events of their lives. May success be yours.

Step 1—Summon your Muse

Before the workshop began, two writing students were into it. "Writing is purely a creative endeavor," Sheila insisted.

"But *screen*writing is a scientific process," Sam argued.

Back and forth they went. Finally, Robert, my teacher's pet, chimed in. "Stop! You're both right. Screenwriting is both an art and a science. The professional writer uses the head as well as the heart."

Sheila and Sam shot doubtful glances. "You can't have it both ways," Sheila replied.

Sure you can, and here's why:

The writing process begins with the creative urge, a desire to express something. Like a tiny seedling, an idea emerges from your heart and pushes its way through the soil of your subconscious. Often, several ideas will sprout. Like any birthing process, this can happen at any time and any place. And with the emergence of your idea comes that wonderful creative feeling.

How do you nurture that young seedling of an idea? What makes it grow? Thought and hard work make it grow. You think about the possibilities. Then, you blueprint the core story, which consists of a beginning, a middle, and an end. All this head work will act like a shot of adrenalin to your heart. More ideas will flow, and the story will evolve until it matures.

Every writer has two natures: the heart and the head. The heart is the passionate creator, the emotional artist, the intuitive subconscious. The head is the detached critic or editor, the logical and analytical scientist or surgeon. And quite conscious.

Good writing utilizes both natures but operates like an alternating current between the two. When you're in the creative, artistic mode, you shut off the head. You encourage the creative flow. You don't correct the spelling or improve the grammar. You just fly. But once that energy is expended, the scientific, critical side takes over and cleans up the mess.

Back and forth you go. You write from the heart. You edit from the head. Back and forth until the head and heart agree (or you've become a schizophrenic).

The good Lord gave our brain two hemispheres. Both are important. Sheila is right-brained and focuses on the intuitive, artistic side of creativity. Sam is left-brained and focuses on the analytical, scientific side of creativity. Each should use his or her greater talent without abandoning his or her lesser talent.

I sometimes worry about writers who search for formulas, who want to make writing purely a science so that they can write by the numbers. They may want inflexible rules so they can be in control of the process. This is to be expected. Our educational system inculcates this into our brains. The secret to great writing is to be part of the process. You can't control it. In truth, the story knows from the beginning where it's going. There is no sweeter moment than when your characters take over and tell you what they want to do and say.

I also worry about the purists who may insist that anything written from the heart is perfect just the way it comes. That which comes easily is not necessarily good. They may be loathe to edit their work for fear of breaking some divine law. If this were true, no one would ever revise anything. There would be no second drafts, no rewriting. So, just because it felt good when you wrote it doesn't mean that it is ready for market.

Writing is an evolutionary process that must be trusted. You must believe that there is a story within you. You must believe that it will find its way out. And you must believe in your talent to nurture it into a stunning script. If you believe, and act on your belief, your Muse will come to you.

THE WRITING PROCESS

Becoming part of the writing process is like "getting religion." For some writers it is almost a mystical experience. Let me provide a suggested framework for this process.

First you start off with a creative jolt, an idea that's about a 7.0 on the Richter scale. Then you do a lot of hard thinking—hammering out a good dramatic premise—beginning, middle, and end. You write the *TV Guide* logline in terms of character, action, opposition, and resolution. What's the concept?

Then, on wings of song, your Muse comes down from Olympus and whispers sweet things. You write all these gems down.

You visualize the one-sheet, the poster that will adorn the movie theater walls in just a couple of years or so. You ask: Do I have a story? Do I have an original concept that will pull people in? If everything feels right up till now, you begin your research.

You develop your characters using both sides of your brain. Remember, even though your characters are within you before you ever begin, once they emerge, they must take on a life of their own.

With an understanding of your story and characters, you now construct the all-important story outline. This outline, sometimes called the step outline, is comprised of paragraphs, one paragraph for each scene, anywhere from 30-100 steps in all. (This figure can vary, depending on genre.) Many writers use 3" x 5" cards, a card for each scene, and pin these cards against the wall. This is when you chart the sequence of your story, alternating between your creative/intuitive nature and your evaluative/practical nature.

Whenever you think you're getting off base, you write a short treatment—about three pages—to get back on track.

By now, your creative pump is primed. You write your first draft from the heart. Some of these scenes are already written from previous bursts of creative joy. Intuitively, creatively, the draft takes shape. The second draft is written from the head, analytically. Death and regeneration.

Even as you approach the end of the process, the story is fluid, evolving into what it eventually wants to be. Don't force the process by being too rigid about scenes you have fallen madly in love with. Don't feel confined by your original outline. Remain open to your Muse.

Now this is just one way to write a script. You will find the way that works best for you with experience. The most important thing is to trust the process and believe in yourself. The story is inside you; you must let it out. So what are you waiting for? Come on. Let's create a masterpiece!

Step 2—Dream up your movie idea

What if you don't have any ideas? Here are a few tips that will help you get those creative juices flowing.

1. Put your mind in a relaxed state through meditation or deep breathing. Visualize a natural setting where you feel safe, or drift off to the setting of your script. The right brain, the Inner Creator, always works best when the left brain, the Inner Critic, has been tranquilized.

2. Rely on the Inspiration Cycle: Input, Incubation, Inspiration, Evaluation. After a few days of jamming your brain, relax and tell yourself you need a breakthrough, then incubate. In other words, wait. It may take a few days. Soon enough, while falling asleep or taking a shower—Eureka!—the inspiration comes. You're flying. It may continue to flow for some time. But don't stop when it does. Evaluate it (the Inner Critic has been waiting for this moment) as a means of bringing on the next cycle of inspiration.

3. Stimulate the senses. Engage in a physical activity such as gardening, chopping wood, shoveling snow, fishing, dancing, aerobics, kneading clay, washing the dishes, tinkering with the car, and so on. Physical activity not only relaxes you, but it stimulates the senses. Being aware of sensory details that will stimulate your writing.

4. Stir your creative desire by inventing writing rituals. Acquire a ball cap and imprint or embroider the word "writer" on it. Whenever it's time to write, you can tell your loved ones, "I'm wearing my writer's cap tonight." I know a writer who begins every session with an herb tea ceremony. Speaking of ceremonies, why not conduct opening and closing ceremonies for the Writer's Olympics, starring you? Writing should be fun, so have a good time.

When I need to drop into the creative mode, I often play stimulating music. Right now it's LES MISERABLES, EDWARD SCISSORHANDS, and JURASSIC PARK, because they stir my emotions and imagination. You may find it helpful to look at a painting, photo, or object that suggests theme, character, or location to you, something that pulls you into your story. I know someone who closes her eyes and types as she visualizes.

5. Reflect on and dip into your past. The research has already been done on your life and your world. It's all inside you. You can draw from this well, especially when you need to feel the emotion your characters are feeling, but beware the quagmires of autobiographical writing.

I'm often asked: Is it true I should write what I know? Can I base my script on something that happened to me years ago? How true to life should my characters be? Can I use myself and people I know? The answer is you need just enough distance from these characters and incidents that they can take on a life of their own.

Writing that is too autobiographical is usually flat, with the central character often becoming an observer of life instead of an active participant. Once I read a script about a wife who was abused by her husband. The wife did nothing but complain for ninty pages. On page 100 a neighbor rescued her. The only reason I read this all the way through was because I was paid to evaluate it. I thought to myself, This is often how real people behave, but movie people are willful and active.

The writer had painted herself into a creative corner. She was too close to the truth. She needed to use the energy of her personal experience and create a drama with it. Even "true" stories combine characters and condense time for dramatic purposes.

The problem with autobiographical writing (and all writing, of course, is partly autobiographical) is that we love our central character. We make her perfect. We're afraid to bloody her nose. Solution? Use yourself and people you know as a basis for the fictional characters you create. Be as autobiographical as you want—you need that energy—but create enough distance to be objective. It's a razor's edge that every writer must walk.

6. Carry around a tape recorder or notebook. (There's never been a writing instructor or adviser who hasn't recommended this helpful tip.) When you carry around a notebook or a microcassette recorder, you are asking your subconscious to find ideas for you. Armed with one of these tools, you'll be more observant and open to wandering ideas looking for a home. Write down, or record, these ideas and bits as they occur to you.

7. See movies in your genre. In fact, see eight good films and two dogs. Read a screenwriting book. Read screenplays—yes!—read screenplays. Page through old movie books or books of foreign films. Attend a seminar or workshop. Remember, don't stop learning in order to write; and don't stop writing in order to learn.

8. Steal. Shakespeare did. Are you greater than he? Look to the classics for plot and character ideas. Creativity is not creating something out of nothing; it's a new twist on an old idea. It's making new combinations of old patterns. It's converting the Big Dipper into the Little Ladle. Creativity is disrupting the regular thought patterns to create a new way of connecting. Gutenberg took the wine press and the coin punch and created the first printing press.

Read fairy tales, folklore, mythology, and history. Many classic plots can be easily adapted. *Romeo and Juliet* became WEST SIDE STORY. *Faust* became DAMN YAN-KEES, ROSEMARY'S BABY, WALL STREET, and BLUE CHIPS. Homer's *Odyssey* became FALLING DOWN. *The Tempest* has been transformed into several movies. How many *Frankenstein* plots can you identify? How about *King Midas, Jack the Giant Killer,* and *Cinderella*/PRETTY WOMAN plots? Maybe it's time for your character to take the Hero's Journey (page 28). Try variations and twists of plots. How about a modern update of *Moby Dick* or some other classic?

9. Visit parks, airports, parties, court rooms, crisis centers or other places where people are likely to congregate or be in some kind of transition. This will help you look for character and story details. You may even find someone to be a character in your script.

10. Read the news. "Giant White Caught Off New England Coast" was the headline that inspired JAWS. "80-Year-Old Widow Weds 17-Year-Old Boy" inspired HAROLD AND MAUDE. TV and radio talk shows can give you ideas for topics that are current.

If you are aware of a true story that would work for a Movie-of-the-Week (and if it's not a big story that has already attracted producer-types), then buy an option to the rights of that story and write the script.

11. Understand dramatic structure. This needs to be said. Sometimes you're stuck because you've violated some principle of dramatic structure. Use this in connection with #7 above. I've heard many writers credit a book or seminar for helping them work through a writing problem.

12. Be open to radical change. Be flexible. I once changed the gender of my central character to awaken a tired story. Maybe you should open your story on your current page 30 instead of page 1. Ask questions. Ask the "what if" question. What if an alien

child was accidentally left behind on Earth? What if my central character's mother is a jackal? Be open to any ideas, and any criticism. Everything goes. Nothing's written in stone until the shoot wraps.

13. Write what you care about, what you have passion for. What type of movie do you like to watch? This may be the type of movie you ought to write. Discover and follow what fascinates you.

Use the energy from pet peeves and gripes. Writing what you feel strongly about will help you keep going when the going gets tough. And keep in mind that the process of writing one script will generate ideas for other scripts and will grease the works for future creative success.

14. Try clustering. It's a technique that naturally summons your creativity and eliminates anxiety. Get a clean sheet of paper and write your story problem, concept, or character about half way down the page. Draw a circle around it.

Now brainstorm, using free association. Whatever comes to mind, write it down, circle it, and connect it to its parent (or simply make a list). Go with any ideas that float by, regardless of how bizarre or strange. Keep your hand moving. If you have a moment when no idea comes, doodle in the corner until it does. Within about five minutes, you'll have a feeling of what you're supposed to do. An insight will come, the solution will be revealed, or a new idea will leap into your mind. If nothing happens, just stay relaxed. This is something that can't be forced.

15. Confront your blocks. List all your barriers to writing and communicate with them; that is, turn your barrier into an object or person and write a dialogue. In this free-writing exercise, an insight will come to you. Yes, you can overcome the barrier.

Keep in mind that the master key to overcoming writer's block is to realize that it's no big deal, just an occupational hazard. The real problem is when you panic. Blocks are just part of the writing process. In fact, a block is a blessing in disguise because now that your "head" is stymied, your subconscious is free to break through. So relax. Have fun. Trust the process.

Once you have a hat full of story ideas, you can search for the nuggets, the genuine movie concepts, the premises that have commercial potential.

CHECKPOINT 1

- How solid is your story idea, premise, or concept?
- Will it appeal to a mass audience?
- Is it fresh? original? provocative? commercial?
- Does hearing it make people say, "I want to see that!"?
- Is it large enough in scope to appear on the silver screen?
- Does it have "legs"—stand on its own as a story without big stars?

CHECKPOINT 2

- Do you have a working title that inspires you?
- Will this title titillate the audience? Is it a "grabber"?
- Does it convey something of your story concept or theme?
- Does it conjure up an image or an emotion?
- Is it short enough to appear on a marquee? (Not always necessary.)

CHECKPOINT 3

Imagine how your movie will be advertised. Then on a sheet of paper, sketch out the one-sheet (movie poster) for your movie.

- Is there a striking visual image that will stop passersby?
- Is there a headline that plays off the title or conveys a high concept?
- Will people want to see this movie?

Step 3—Develop Your Core Story

What is your story about? You need to know this and you need to know it now. There are producers who believe that if you can't tell them your story in a sentence or two, there isn't a story. They may be right.

A story presents a character who wants something and who is opposed by at least one other character. This opposition causes conflict and a series of critical events all leading to the Crisis and Showdown at the end. Here are the critical events in virtually all dramas and comedies:

CATALYST

Your story starts out in balance, but the Catalyst upsets that balance (hopefully by page 10-15), giving the central character a desire, problem, need, goal, mission, or something to do. The story now has direction and movement. In WITNESS, the catalyst is the Amish boy witnessing the murder. It gives Harrison Ford something to do—try to find the killer.

BIG EVENT

This is an event that changes your central character's life in a big way, thus the Big Event. It comes in around pages 20-30. This is where Marty travels to 1955 in BACK TO THE FUTURE.

PINCH

About half way through the script, there is another major plot twist. It is often a point of no return for the central character, or the moment when the character becomes fully committed, or when the motivation is strengthened or becomes clear. It's when Scarlet O'Hara vows never to go hungry again in GONE WITH THE WIND.

CRISIS

This is an event that forces a crucial decision. Often it is simply the low point in the story, the moment when all looks lost, or when the lovers are separated. In E.T., it's when the men converge on the house and E.T. is dying. How will he ever get home now? In about 15-30 pages, we'll find out.

SHOWDOWN

Commonly called the climax, this is when the central character and opposition character square off. It's the final battle in STAR WARS, the breakfast-table scene in MOONSTRUCK.

REALIZATION

Just after the Showdown, or during it, or occasionally before it, the audience realizes that your central character has grown, changed, or figured something out. This is when the scarecrow asks Dorothy what she has learned. She knows now that there's no place like home. It's when the family admires and accepts Kevin at the end of HOME ALONE. Let's look at examples from four movies.

DAVE

Catalyst:	Dave is asked to pretend he's president
Big Event:	The real president dies; Dave "becomes" president
Pinch:	Dave acts as president and defies the press secretary
Crisis:	The press secretary implicates Dave in a scandal
Showdown:	Dave defeats the press secretary at a joint session of Congress
Realization:	I can *help people find jobs*. —Dave runs for office

THELMA & LOUISE

Catalyst: Louise takes Thelma fishing
Big Event: Louise shoots and kills Thelma's attacker
Pinch: Louise tells Jimmy good-bye
Crisis: It becomes apparent that Thelma and Louise will die
Showdown: They are pursued to the Grand Canyon—there's a standoff at the rim
Realization: We've *achieved a certain freedom together.*

TWINS

Catalyst: Danny meets his brother Arnold
Big Event: Danny is saved by his brother, so he takes him in
Pinch: Danny meets the scientist; believes Arnold really is his brother
Crisis: Danny must choose between his brother and $5 million
Showdown: Together, Danny and Arnold trick the bad guy
Realization: *I'm not genetic garbage.* —Danny finds his mother

THE HAND THAT ROCKS THE CRADLE

	Peyton (Central Character)	Claire (Protagonist)
Catalyst:	Hub's suicide; no family	Molested by doctor
Big Event:	Gets Claire to hire her	Hires Peyton
Pinch:	Gets Solomon kicked out	Fires Solomon
Crisis:	Kicked out of the house	Asthma attack
Showdown:	Battle with Claire	Battle with Peyton
Realization:	None	*I trust my instincts.* (Trusts Solomon w/child)

CHECKPOINT 4

Write the *TV Guide* logline for your story.

- Who is your central character?
- What is his/her main goal? (This is the goal that drives the story.)
- Why is the goal so important to him/her?
- Who is trying to stop your character from achieving the goal?

CHECKPOINT 5

Identify the parameters of your story.

- What is the genre? (Action/adventure, thriller, romantic comedy, etc.)
- What is the time and setting?
- What is the emotional atmosphere, and the mood?
- What, if any, story or character limits exist?

CHECKPOINT 6

- What is the Catalyst that gives your central character a direction?
- What Big Event really impacts your character's life?
- Is there a strong, rising conflict throughout Act 2?
- Does the conflict build? or just become repetitive?
- Is there a Pinch, a twist in the middle, that divides Act 2 in half and more fully motivates your character?
- What terrible Crisis will your character face?
- Will the Crisis force a life/death decision, and/or make the audience fret about how things will turn out in the end?
- How does your story end? What is the Showdown?
- In the end, does your character learn something new?
    - Or, is his/her growth (positive or negative) made apparent?
    - Or, does he/she receive any recognition in the end?

CHECKPOINT 7

Now write out your core story in three paragraphs, one for the beginning, one for the middle, and one for the end. Paragraph 1 will end with the Big Event; paragraph 2 with the Crisis. Obviously, you cannot include all of the characters in this brief synopsis. Once this is done, re-evaluate your story.

Step 4—Create your movie people

Your central character wants something specific. That something is the goal. The character, who is conscious of this desire, strives for it throughout most of the story. Of course, the character is opposed by at least one other person.

In most stories, the character also has an inner need, something she may not be consciously aware of until the Crisis. This need is a yearning for the one thing that will bring true happiness or fulfillment to the character. The need is blocked by a flaw, usually a form of selfishness. The flaw emerges from a past traumatic event—the backstory.

The main plot of most movies is driven by the goal. It's the Outside/Action Story.

The main subplot is driven by the need. It's the Inside/Emotional Story. It is usually focused on the primary relationship in the story. It's concerned with character dynamics.

The Outside/Action Story is the spine; it holds things together. The Inside/Emotional Story is the heart; it touches the audience. To make the Outside/Action Story and Inside/Emotional Story work, you need to understand your movie people and how they function.

CHECKPOINT 8

Does your central character have the following?

- An outside goal that the audience will care about?
- A powerful, personal motivation for achieving the goal?
- An opposition character in a position of strength, capable of doing great damage?
- The will to act against opposition, and to learn and grow?
- Human emotions, traits, values, and imperfections that people can identify with?

- A particular point of view of life, the world, and/or self, giving rise to attitudes?
- Details, extensions, idiosyncracies, and/or expressions that are uniquely his/hers?
- A life and voice (dialogue) of his/her own?
- A key event from the past that has given rise to a character flaw?
- An inner need that he/she may be unaware of at first?

CHECKPOINT 9

Evaluate your other main characters (and especially your opposition character) by the criteria of Checkpoint 8. Each should have at least a goal or intention in the story. The more depth you can give them, the more interesting they will appear.

CHECKPOINT 10

Your movie people have sociological, psychological, and physiological characteristics. Use the following to provoke your creative thought.

Sociology

Occupation	Education	Criminal record
Birthplace/upbringing	Ethnic roots	Religion
Past/present home life	Political views	Social status
Hobbies	Affiliations	Private life
Work history	Work environment	Personal life

Physiology

Height/weight	Build or figure	Attractiveness
Appearance	Hair/eyes	Voice quality
Defects/scars	Health/strength	Complexion
Clothing	Physical skills	Athletic ability

Psychology

Fears/phobias	Secrets	Attitudes
Prejudices	Values/beliefs	Inhibitions
Pet peeves	Complexes	Addictions
Superstitions	Habits	Moral stands
Ambitions	Motivations	Temperament
Personal problems	Imagination	Likes/dislikes
Intelligence	Disposition	

CHECKPOINT 11

These are questions to ask of any of your movie people:

- How do you handle stress, pressure, relationships, problems, emotion?
- Are you extroverted or shy? intuitive or analytical? active or passive?
- What's your most traumatic experience? most thrilling experience?
- Essentially, who are you? What is at your core?
- What is your dominant trait?
- What do you do and think when you're alone and no one will know?
- How do you feel about yourself?
- How do you feel about the other people in the story?
- Who are the most important people in your life?
- How do you relate to each?
- What's the worst (and best) thing that could happen to you?
- What are you doing tonight? tomorrow?
- Where do you want to be ten years from now?

CHECKPOINT 12

- How does your central character grow or change throughout the story?
- How is your character different at the end of the story?
- What does he/she know at the end that he/she did not know at the beginning?
- What is your character's perception of reality?
- Does that perception change by the end of the story?
- Is your protagonist likeable?
- Will the audience identify with your central character on some level?
- Does your central character have depth, with both strengths and weaknesses?
- Will the two key roles attract stars?

CHECKPOINT 13

- What is the theme or message of your story?
- What are you trying to say?
- Will the end of your story say it for you without being preachy?
  (The theme may not be evident to you until later in your writing.)

CHECKPOINT 14

Revise your three-paragraph synopsis to incorporate any changes to your story.

Step 5—Step out your story

This is where you find out if your story is going to work or not. Here, you outline your story. This work will make the actual writing much easier than it would ordinarily be.

CHECKPOINT 15

Plot the action of your story. Identify your central character's action plot and emotional subplot. Look at your other movie people; identify their goals. Their goals will drive their individual plots (actually subplots). Do these various plot lines intersect, resulting in adequate conflict for drama or comedy?

CHECKPOINT 16

Write a four-page treatment (double-spaced). Summarize the beginning of your story in one page, the middle in two pages, and the end in one page. Focus on two to four main characters, the key events (plot points), and the emotional undercurrent of the story. Although somewhat difficult, this exercise will help tremendously in laying a strong foundation for your story. Now answer these questions.

- Is the central conflict of the story clearly defined?
- Are the character's goal and need clear?
- Are the stakes of the story big enough for a commercial movie?
- Does the story evoke an emotional response?
- Will the audience cry, get angry, laugh, get scared, fall in love, get excited, etc.?
- What makes this story unique, fresh, and original?
- Is your story too predictable? Have we seen this before?
- Are the facts of the story plausible? (They don't have to be possible, just plausible.)
- Will people be emotionally satisfied at the end?

CHECKPOINT 17

Step out your script. This is a crucial step. Traditionally, the step outline consists of a series of 3" x 5" cards, one card for each scene or dramatic unit. Consider attaching these cards (or post-it notes) to a wall, table, or cork board to see the entire story at once.

At the top of each card write the master scene heading, then summarize the action of the scene in a sentence or short paragraph, emphasizing the essential action and purpose of the scene. Some writers like to list the characters appearing in the scene in the lower left-hand corner of the card. That way, they can see who is where at a glance.

You can use the lower right-hand corner for pacing and tracking plots. Some writers use a highlighter and identify plots by color. Blue is the action story, red is the love story, and so on.

You can identify scenes as fast or slow, action or dialogue. If you discover that you have four dialogue scenes in a row, all with the same characters, you can adjust this pacing problem by moving scenes around, cross-cutting with action scenes, condensing, or even omitting an unnecessary scene.

If additional ideas come to you, jot them down on blank cards. You'll end up with 30-100 cards, depending on the nature of the story.

Of course, you don't have to use 3" x 5" cards. You can step-out your story on your computer—whatever works for you. Once completed, your step outline will become the basis for writing your script.

CHECKPOINT 18

Now that your step outline is complete, ask yourself these questions:

- Are your scenes well paced?
- Do the major turning points come at about the right time?
- Do things just happen, or is there a cause-and-effect relationship between character actions?
- Do the subplots intersect with the main plot, creating new complications?
- Are your characters' actions motivated, or do they exist just to make the story work?
- Does action, conflict, and dramatic tension build, or just repeat and become static?
- Are your central and opposition characters forced to take stronger and stronger actions?
- Does the conflict rise naturally to a crisis/climax?

Step 6—Write your first draft

Write your first draft from the heart. Keep your head out of it as much as possible. It's okay to change the story. It's okay to overwrite. It's okay to include too much dialogue. Everything goes, everything flows.

Once this draft is completed, you may wish to register it with the Writers Guild of America. This is optional since you will register it again after your final polish.

CHECKPOINT 19

It is absolutely imperative that you do the following upon completion of the first draft.

1. Take at least two weeks off from your script. Let it ferment for a while. You will be much more objective for the pre-revision analysis (Checkpoints 20-24). During this time you may want to read a book, go to a seminar, see movies of the same genre, or read scripts, or turn your attention to other things.

2. Reward yourself in some way that makes you feel good about yourself.

Step 7—Make the necessary revisions

Before writing the second draft, consider letting your hot property cool off. Sit on it a couple of weeks, then craft your second draft from your head. Here, you become a script surgeon. Whittle down the dialogue; remove unnecessary narration, flashbacks, dream sequences, and so on. You become an analyst in every way you can define that word. Once this work is completed, polish your script until you are ready to present your wonder to Hollywood. The following checkpoints will help you evaluate your revisions.

CHECKPOINT 20

Review Checkpoints 1-19. Do not skip this checkpoint.

CHECKPOINT 21 (the script itself)

- Is your script too technical, too complex, or too difficult to understand?
- Will your script require a huge budget with unshootable scenes, such as herds of camels crossing the San Diego Freeway? Other possible big budget problems: Special effects, period settings, exotic locations, too many arenas or locations, large cast, water, and animals.
- Is your script's budget about right for its market?
- Have you followed the rules of formatting and presentation as described in Book III?
- Have you written thoughts, feelings, memories, or anything else that cannot appear on the screen?

CHECKPOINT 22 (dialogue)

- Is the dialogue "too on the nose"?
- Do your characters say exactly what they feel?
- Does each character speak with his/her own voice, vocabulary, slang, rhythm, and style?
- Is the dialogue crisp, original, clever, compelling, and lean?
- Are individual speeches too long or encumbered with more than one thought?
- Does the story rely too heavily on dialogue?
- Are your dialogue scenes too long?
- Are there too many scenes with talking heads?
- Are you telling when you could be showing?
- Is the comedy *trying* to be funny, or is it naturally funny?

CHECKPOINT 23 (exposition)

- Are you boring your audience by telling too much too soon?
- Are you confusing your audience with too little information?
- Are you giving your audience just enough exposition to keep them on the edge of their seats?
- Is your exposition revealed through conflict or through static dialogue?
- Have you used flashbacks as a crutch or as a means to move the story forward?

CHECKPOINT 24 (character and story)

- Will the reader root for your hero?
- Will the reader have an emotional identification with the hero?
- Are your characters believable? Are they humans with dimension?
- Do your characters come across as retreads whom we've seen before?
- Do any of your characters grow or change throughout the story?
- Is there a moment at the end when this growth will be recognized by the reader?
- When will the reader cry?
- Is the story too gimmicky, relying too heavily on nudity, violence, shock, or special effects?
- Will the first five to ten pages capture the reader's interest?
- Do the first twenty to thirty pages set up the central conflict?
- Does the middle build in intensity toward the Showdown at the end?
- Is the story, plot, or ending too predictable?
- Are all the loose ends tied up in the denouement (the resolution after the Showdown)?

CHECKPOINT 25

Sometimes it just doesn't work. You have story problems, character problems, and you're not quite sure how to solve them. When you are blocked or you sense something is wrong, what can you do?

1. Don't panic. We all go through this. Realize that you have the ability to solve your problems.

2. Take two weeks off. Don't worry about it. You may get inspiration during this period because you will be more relaxed.

3. Read a book; go to a seminar; flick out. Many of my "breakthroughs" have come on the plane while reading a book about writing.

4. Often you actually know where the trouble is. You have a gnawing feeling inside about something in your story, or perhaps a sense that "something" is wrong, but you ignore it because you don't want to do a major rewrite. In my script-analysis work, I don't know how many times a writer has told me the following: "I kinda knew what was wrong, but I guess I needed you to confirm it." The point is this: You have an inner sense that you must learn to trust, even when it makes the writing process uncomfortable and the rewriting painful.

5. Get feedback from other writers or professionals.

6. Study mythology (Christopher Vogler's *Writer's Journey*) and understand your genre.

7. Revise your four-page treatment. Sometimes this helps you get back on track.

8. Create a Character/Action Grid. Essentially, this is a mini step outline, constructed on one or two sheets of paper. Across the top of the page, list your five to seven main characters. These are your columns. Below each name, identify each character's purpose in the story, goal, motivation, and/or any other parameters you'd like. Just taking the exercise this far may reveal some problems.

Then write brief descriptions of each scene under each character's name and step out your script. This way, you can see character actions crisscrossing throughout the story. You will find an example of a Character/Action Grid on the next page. This example is not complete. You will want to list every important action of five to seven characters from the beginning to the end of the script.

Example of the Character/Action Grid

JIM	SALLY	MAX
Central character/hero	Love interest, 2nd opp.	Main opposition
Investigative journalist	Animal-rights advocate	Circus owner
Goal: Exploit Blimpo the Elephant for a story	Save Blimpo the Elephant from exploitation	#1 Circus Act in U.S.
Motivation: Salvage career	Blimpo saves her (later)	Prove he's not a loser
Need: Be more caring	Trust and love Jim	Respect animals
Flaw: Anything for a story	Only trusts animals	Inhumane

ACTIONS:
Fired: Then gets last chance
Dumped by Sally   Dumps Jim; can't trust

                                                Max whips Blimpo
                Kidnaps Blimpo; chased   Chases Sally
                Hides Blimpo in Jim's yard
Morning: Finds Blimpo

Continue outlining your characters' actions to the end. When the grid is completed, you will be able to see your entire story on one or two pages. The structure, pacing, motivation, and plot lines will be easier to work with.

CHECKPOINT 26

Before you submit your script, do the following:

- Get feedback from writers' group members.
- Consider hiring a professional reader or script analyst.
- Review Checkpoints 1-24 one last time.
- Make adjustments. Is your script a "good read"?
- Be sure the script looks 100% professional and that it is formatted correctly.
- Register your script with the Writers Guild of America.
- Create a marketing success plan (see Book IV).

HOW TO SELL YOUR SCRIPT

BOOK IV

A Marketing Plan

Congratulations! You, the next great screenwriter, have written a stunning script! Realize that you have reached a major milestone. You should definitely reward yourself with positive self-talk and a bowl of ice cream.

There are several markets for scripts, and we will discuss them all. But before you even think of approaching the marketplace, you want to get your ducks in a row. I have watched with sadness the many writers who have broken their hearts by approaching the market prematurely. Here's how to prepare.

How to protect your work

In Hollywood, no script is sacred. Don't worry, there are ways to protect you and your creative offspring. There are ways to protect your rights.

Keep records
First, be organized. Life can get very complicated, so write things down. Keep a journal of meetings you have with people and record what was discussed. Keep a log of phone calls, queries, and script submissions. You'll need these for the lawsuit later. You'll also use these records to follow up on contacts and create future strategies for selling your work.

If there's ever any question in your mind that there might be a legal problem, consult an entertainment attorney. You may even want an attorney to review any contracts you're offered, particularly if the offerer is not signatory to the Writers Guild of America.

Note: Only attorneys can give legal advice, and I am therefore not qualified to do so. Nothing in this volume should be construed as legal advice because it is not intended as such.

Copyright

Keep in mind that there are certain things you cannot protect: Ideas, historical facts, plots, titles, phrases, and anything not written down. Here's what you can protect: Your original expression of an idea or plot; in other words, your original, spec script is the only thing you can protect. A spec script is a screenplay written on the speculation that someone will buy it later; writing such a screenplay will help protect your idea.

There are several ways to protect your spec screenplay. Under the new copyright law, you own the copyright to your work even as you write it. You don't even need to use the copyright symbol. To create a public record of your script, however, you may wish to *register* your copyright with the U.S. Copyright Office in Washington, D.C. It's a simple, painless, and inexpensive procedure. Just contact the Copyright Office in Washington, D.C. Once done, you must display the copyright symbol on your script.

My personal observation is that most writers do not register their scripts with the copyright office, presumably because the eventual producer will own the copyright to the completed film, and thus the script. That doesn't mean that *you* shouldn't. After all, registering your copyright gives you the best protection you can get.

The WGA and other means of protection

The purpose of registration is to establish yourself as the creator of your original work. Most writers register their scripts with the Writers Guild of America. All nine of my scripts are registered with the WGA only. I don't want a script dated—they get old fast, and the copyright symbol dates the script. No matter what protective methods you use, make sure one of them is registration with the Writers Guild of America.

The Writers Guild maintains two offices. One is in Los Angeles; the other is in New York.

To register your script with the WGA, simply send your screenplay, treatment, or synopsis to them with $20 ($22 for the Writers Guild, east) and they will hold the copy for five years. It can be retrieved at any time thereafter. When five years have expired, you may renew your registration. You may register your script more than once. Some writers like to register their first draft as well as their final polish. You only need to register a treatment or synopsis if you are going to present it to others, or if you're going to delay the writing of your script.

An alternative to the Writers Guild registration service is that provided by the recently formed National Creative Registry. They will register your script for a lower fee than the WGA. To date, the WGA has not stated whether or not they'd recognize a National Creative Registry registration in cases where the WGA must arbitrate a credits dispute between writers. I suspect they would, but that remains to be seen. (The National Creative Registry is also listed in Book V.)

Another way to protect your work is to have several people read it so that they can testify that you wrote it.

Still another method is the Poor Man's Copyright. (I suppose if you're a poor woman, it can work for you as well.) Put the script in an envelope, seal it, and send it via *registered mail* to yourself. Don't open it; keep it for the lawsuit later.

The Writers Guild provides other services to writers besides their script registration service. You do not need to belong the Guild to benefit from their services, or to register your script.

What can the WGA offer you? Here's a list of services.

- Registration of your script, treatment, or synopsis for a period of five years. You may renew your registration after that.

- Pre-negotiated contracts if you sign with a producer or studio that is signatory to the Guild or acquire an agent who is signatory to the Guild.

- Arbitration if a dispute arises regarding credits or for other grievances.

- A list of agencies that are signatory to the Guild. The cost is nominal.

- A library where you can go and read scripts.

- Information as to who represents a particular writer. This could help in your search for an agent.

Again, you need not be a member to use these services. You may join the Guild once you have the required number of credits. For more information, contact the appropriate office. Refer to Book V for addresses and phone numbers. Remember, The Mississippi River serves as the boundary between the jurisdictions of the east and west Guild offices.

What you must do before entering the market

To break into this business, you need at least one showcase script (preferably two or more) that is proof of your writing ability. If you want to write for television, you will need one feature script and at least one sample television script.

This showcase script (or scripts) should be registered with the Writers Guild, formatted correctly, and should be complete in every way. Never submit a work in progress. The script must be as good as it can be. Realize that your script is a prospectus asking for a $10-30 million investment. That is why it must be good.

Since Tinsel Town is into appearances, it is essential that your script look as good as it can possibly look. Obviously, you will want to format it correctly, avoiding camera directions and editing directions (unless it is a script for animation). You may wonder why I'm against technical directions when most scripts you've read have them. That's because most scripts you've read are *shooting* scripts.

The neophyte seldom sees the *selling* script or *spec* script. That's the script you're writing. (See Book II for a spec-script style guide.) A spec script is lean on actor's instruction, or *wrylies*. These are the parentheticals that appear after the character's name and before the character's dialogue. Your spec script must provide a good *read*. You want a narrative flow that is unencumbered by camera directions, editing directions, and other technical intrusions. After the script's sold, the director and others will turn it into the shooting script.

To further guide you in preparing a professional-looking script, there's a list of twelve common errors on page 66. Many of the points seem nit-picky. They are, and for good reason. The poor souls who must read dozens of scripts every week are looking for any excuse to eliminate scripts from their reading stack. Abiding by their simple rules is an easy way to make a good impression.

Of course, appearance isn't everything, and correct format alone will not save you. Your script must tell an interesting story. It must be well-crafted. There can be no references to the thoughts and feelings of characters: *When John saw Mary, it reminded him of the first time they met.* Don't write anything that cannot appear on the screen. You are limited in your writing to what can be *seen*, and what can be *heard*. That's it.

Your description should focus on images and actions; your dialogue should be crisp and allow for subtext. The writing in general should be concrete, specific, and clear. Consulting Book II will help your writing style as well as your formatting technique.

Before submitting your script, you may wish to get feedback. Perhaps, the best place for that is through a writers' group. I recommend writers groups of about seven to ten writers who meet regularly and read each other's work. You will get worthwhile feedback and the advice will be free.

WRITERS' GROUPS

Writing can be a lonely job. A writers' group may be just the place to turn for comfort, support, and feedback.

Where to find writers' groups
Writers' groups are everywhere if you know where to look. Here are six general areas to begin your search.

1. Attend writers' conferences, workshops, and writing classes. Network with fellow writers and ask them if they know of any writers' groups.

2. Read the classified ads of writing publications. Many groups and individuals advertise in the classifieds, seeking to form or continue a group. Some established groups, like the Screenwriter's Network in Los Angeles, have special requirements.

3. For a fee, you may join large, professional organizations such as The Screenwriter's Network (already mentioned), the National Writer's Club (303/751-7844), the Hawaii Screenwriter's Association (free membership), and the Wisconsin Screenwriter's Forum. (See listings in Book V.)

4. Call your state film commissioner or county film board (if one exists) about possible writers' groups in your area.

5. Other places where writers might hang out include film festivals, movie clubs, bookstores, and university and adult education programs.

6. Don't forget to approach nonwriting friends and acquaintances who might know writers who belong to groups.

If your search for a writers' group proves fruitless, there's only one thing left to do—start your own group.

How to find writers to start a group
You know now where writers can be found. Here are ways to gather them into a group.

1. Network with them at conferences and workshops. Trade phone numbers. One writer recently used this simple, proven method to create a group composed of participants of my seminar and Michael Hauge's.

2. Ask the instructor to put your name and phone number on the board because you'd like to start a writers' group. That way interested writers can call you.

3. Post a notice on bulletin boards and classrooms at conferences, asking people to sign up. You can pick these lists up later.

4. Distribute flyers to classmates or fellow conference-goers. You can even go out on a limb and announce the first meeting in the flyer.

5. Place a "Writers Wanted" classified ad in scriptwriting newsletters and magazines (see Book V for a list of periodicals).

6. Send a letter of invitation to college or adult-education classes, announcing the date of your meeting.

7. Try bulletin boards and round tables featured in on-line computer services such as GEnie, America Online, and CompuServe. Surf the Internet.

How to keep the group going
While you're forming the group, you will want to create some rules or guidelines at the same time. Here are some things to keep in mind.

Include writers that are at basically the same level. One group might consist of people who are just getting started. Another group might set up a requirement of one completed screenplay.

Keep the group small. Five people may be enough. Seven is an ideal size. If you start with twelve to fifteen people, you'll likely end up with the magnificent seven who are dedicated.

Make it a participative group. You may need a facilitator to head the group, but make sure everyone has an equal say in making rules. You might even rotate responsibilities, such as making reminder calls and assigning refreshments, so that no one is unduly burdened and everyone is involved.

Find a place to meet. This will probably be someone's house. It might be easier to use the same location continuously, but some groups like to rotate. Many libraries, savings-and-loan associations, and other businesses have "community rooms" that are without cost for noncommercial use. You qualify if admittance to your group is free.

Have a regular meeting time, such as the first Tuesday of every month, or every Wednesday at 7:30. Get people into a routine.

Decide on the purposes of the group. For example, here is the stated purpose of a group of my students: "To provide each member with the feedback he or she needs to forward his or her screenwriting career. Group members share screenwriting knowledge and provide friendly, constructive critiques of each other's script, treatment, or outline. Members also exchange screenwriting books, magazines, tapes, and their experiences finding agents and marketing scripts."

Some groups focus on one or two writers per session. Some groups require members to send the work to others in advance of the meetings. It's often profitable to read scenes aloud at the meeting itself and evaluate them on the spot, or discuss writing ideas and specific writing problems.

Make sure critiquing sessions do not turn into slugfests. Writers should avoid a defensive posture. Listen carefully, avoid speaking, take the advice seriously, but remember that you are the writer of *your* script. Criticism should be given constructively. Members should avoid speaking in absolutes, but instead offer their opinions, reactions, observations, and suggestions.

Each member should agree to a code of silence. Everything discussed or read is confidential.

How to creatively maintain your group
After a while, a motivating routine develops into a fatiguing rut. Since all members of the group are *creative*, this problem can be solved by being creative. Here are some ideas to get you started.

- Organize a script swap night

- Read a script, then view the movie together

- Sponsor a contest, or challenge another group to a contest

- Compile a collection of query letters or rejection letters

- Have special awards when a writer passes a milestone

- Set aside a night just for pitching practice; rotate the roles of writer and producer/executive

When groups get too large, create specialized areas such as the "Comedy Writers," or the "Sci-Fi Chapter," and so on. You can have a short, large meeting for everyone, and then break into the specialized groups.

In the best writers' groups and organizations, a feeling of comraderie develops, enabling each writer to root for the other's success. It's an upward spiral of positive energy that revitalizes each writer. This is the fuel each writer needs to keep writing.

OTHER WAYS TO GET FEEDBACK

Some writers seek out a professional reader for a coverage. A coverage is what a reader (actual title is *story analyst*) writes for the agents, producers, and executives who hire her. It usually consists of a two-page synopsis, a brief analysis of the screenplay, and a recommendation. The cost for such a coverage is around $50-100.

More extensive than a coverage is a detailed evaluation provided by professional script consultants like myself. That's going to cost you more. Check the listings in Book V for both story analysts and script consultants.

Another way to get feedback is to ask your spouse and friends to read your script. And we know what that's worth.

ATTITUDE

Success in the marketplace requires a certain mind-set. Realize that the writing business is just that—a business. You want to be professional in your dealings with others. Be confident without being arrogant, and wily without being devious. It's easy to be intimidated by these "glamorous" people, but in reality they are no different from you, except that they have a different job.

Today's screenwriter needs to be enthusiastic and pleasantly persistent. I've seen very talented writers fall by the wayside, and mediocre writers make it because they were persistent. You must be committed.

People want to work with writers they can "work with." This is you if you can stand back from your work and be objective about it. It's difficult taking criticism, particularly mindless criticism, but being defensive will work against you whether you are right or wrong. At the same time, you must believe in your work and be excited about it. After all, if you don't believe in it, who will?

Confidence, conviction, and initiative are pluses. Arrogance, conceit, and passivity are minuses.

Don't count on hitting a home run on the first pitch. You are probably not going to get a million dollars for your first spec script, although it has happened. Allow yourself to be realistic without being negative. Be prepared to walk this road one step at a time without appearing too hungry along the way.

Also, make an inventory of your strengths and the strengths of your script. Be able to tell your story—or present a story hook—in twenty-five words or less. More about pitching and queries later.

Four effective marketing strategies for a fast start

Okay, your script is as good as it can be. You've integrated any feedback that you've received. Your script looks professional. It is registered with the Guild. You, the next great screenwriter, are ready to present your wonder to the world.

REFERRALS AND NETWORKING

The best way to sell your script is by referral to someone in the business. Take some time to list all the people you know who are in the business. Then list anyone you know who you think might know someone in the industry. This will be a much longer list.

My students are always surprised at the results of this powerful little exercise. Once they mention to friends, acquaintances, and relatives that they are writing a script, the windows of heaven often open before them, and blessings pour down on their heads.

You may discover that your Aunt Tilly once dated Dabney Coleman, or that your friend was a fraternity brother of Brad Pitt, or that your boss was a childhood playmate of Goldie Hawn.

Take the time to ask around. This list of potential contacts could include producers, executives, actors, directors, script supervisors, assistants-to-whomever, agents, gophers, gaffers, grips, secretaries, and even janitors. Yes, even gaffers and janitors are insiders. You will be surprised at how close to the action a gaffer (or any hired hand) can get you.

Once you have a list of names, contact them by phone, fax, or mail. The first words out of your mouth or on the letter will be the name of the person who referred you.

Then simply ask this contact to read your script. Tell him you'd love to get his opinion. I am always surprised at how generous people are in these situations. Since producers and agents often receive over 100 scripts a week, it can be difficult getting your script to someone, and yet that same person may readily accept a referred script and place it at the top of their pile.

If your contact enjoys the read, he will know what to do with the script and whom to give it to. If your contact is a producer, she will refer you to an agent so that the script can be "legally" submitted. Sometimes the script will be referred to another Hollywood-type person. I've heard of assistants and mail boys just placing the script on someone's desk. Someone may even want to "discover" you.

One surprised student reported that she mentioned her script to a relative who happened to know a TV producer. This TV producer read the script and referred her to an agent. Now she is a working writer.

Don't think that the only possibilities lie in Hollywood. You might have opportunities in your own area. There are many regional production companies, and there are film people in every state.

CONTESTS

Another marketing ploy is to enter a contest. A list of these is provided in Book V. Also be aware of local contests. Again, contact your state film commissioner about opportunities for screenwriters.

Even if you don't win a contest, scripts are often judged by, or otherwise find their way to, industry professionals. You might make a contact, get a meeting, or even receive an offer. In fact, entering contests can be done concurrently with your other selling efforts.

In entering contests, be sure to read the rules carefully. Most contests have their own formatting requirements and some may be looking for specific types of scripts. Many will state their judging criteria. Make sure your script is polished before you submit it.

If you win a contest or place, you can insert this fact in the qualifications section of your query letter. You have more credibility now; plus you've achieved a milestone that can give you momentum and energy on your upward climb. I've had several students win or place in contests; one had an agent and major studio deal within three days of winning the Nicholl.

ACT AS A PRODUCER

Perhaps the best way to break into Movies-of-the-Week (MOW) and other markets is by finding a true story and acquiring the rights to that story. Do not look for front-page stories that are well-known—those rights are tied up before the ink dries on the newspaper article. And, on the other side of the coin, no one wants to know how your Uncle Bob went mad.

Look for personal stories of individuals battling against impossible odds. If you find such a story, consult an entertainment attorney. You will probably be advised to buy an option to the rights. Here is how such an option would work.

You pay a small amount of money—it could be $20 or $2,000—for the exclusive rights to the person's life or story for a period of time, hopefully several years. During that *option period*, you control the rights to that story, and you alone have the option of buying the rights outright. The actual purchase price for the rights will be a much larger figure, maybe ten or twenty times the option amount.

During the option period, you will write the script and then approach MOW producers. You can more easily hook a producer because you have a script in hand, not simply because own the rights to a true story. When the producer buys your script, he will also pay for the rights. If you fail to secure a deal before the option period expires, the rights revert back to the owner, and the owner keeps your option payment as well.

Now let's suppose you want to acquire the rights to a novel. You will contact the subsidiary rights department of the book publisher, or hire an entertainment attorney to do this for you. Again, you will want to buy an option to the rights of the book. That way, you only tie up a little money but still control the rights for a period of time. You must now write the script and sell it before the deadline of the option agreement.

Keep in mind TROTTIER RULE #9: Don't adapt it until you own it. You will only get hurt and waste time if you write a script on something you don't own. Don't write the sequel to anything unless you control the rights. Don't use a song as the basis of your screenplay unless you own the rights to the music.

When you buy rights or an option to the rights of anything, be sure your attorney verifies copyright, and that there are no liens or encumbrances attached to the work.

Don Moriarty and Greg Alt played it smart. They got their start by buying the rights to the book *The Mark of Zorro*. Then they wrote a screenplay entitled ZORRO, THE COMEDY ADVENTURE, which evolved into ZORRO, THE GAY BLADE. They were able to attract a producer because they owned the rights to the book.

What about writing about famous people? First, consult an entertainment attorney. Second, don't assume anything. Third, don't write anything until you control the rights. As a general rule, if the person has exploited his life by granting interviews or running for office, etc., then he is fair game—probably. You don't want to run the risk of lawsuits or a libel charge, so consult an attorney before proceeding. Truth is a defense of libel so long as there is an absence of malice. (Sounds like a movie I saw.) History, of course, is in the public domain.

If you *base* your story on real people or a real incident, just make sure your script is totally fictitious. If your script is based on a real person, and if that person's peers can deduce from the movie who the movie is about, then that could be invasion of privacy.

My advice is to avoid anything that could possibly get you into a legal entanglement. You should think twice even about buying an option to the rights to a book or someone's story. Make sure you want to make the financial investment.

If an attorney misrepresents you, then see the State Bar. If you stop using an attorney, he must turn over his files to you.

BECOME A STORY ANALYST

Why not become a reader? Readers, officially known as *story analysts*, make Hollywood go around. No one reads any more except readers. Agents and producers alike hire readers to read the huge volume of submitted scripts. The reader will *cover* the script; that is, write *coverage*, consisting of a synopsis, evaluation, and recommendation. The coverage is about four pages in length.

You can become a reader, meet Hollywood types, and learn a lot from reading the work of other writers. The pay is low, from zero to $80 a script. You'll need to live near your employer's office—they often want scripts read overnight. You get hired by presenting a sample coverage and any credentials to agencies and production companies.

OTHER MARKETING STRATEGIES

Obviously, these are not the only strategies open to you. You can seek an agent, sell the script yourself to producers or talent, or you can enter Hollywood through the back door. We'll discuss each of these strategies at length.

How to find an agent

As you might guess, there are many advantages to acquiring an agent. Agents save you time. They know the territory and how to negotiate a deal. Because agents are expected by the industry to screen out crummy writers, the fact you have one greatly multiplies your chances of finding work. Best of all, agents don't cost anything until they sell your script. Some large agencies, such as ICM and CAA, package scripts; that is, they add talent or a director to generate a studio deal. They are generally more difficult to break into than small agencies. Although a small agency may be a better choice for the novice, you want whomever you can get!

You may have heard how difficult it is to get read. First of all, it is true that agents will seldom read your script, but their assistants will *if* the agent is properly approached.

First, secure a list of approved agencies from the Writers Guild. Their list is coded so that you can select the agencies that are accepting submissions. Keep in mind that the Guild lists agencies, but not individual agents. For this, you may need to go to a directory. I recommend the agent's directory put out by Hollywood Creative Directories (listed in Book V).

Study the various agency lists and directories you have acquired. If using a directory, you will single out the literary agent that is the farthest down the list in a given agency. As a last resort, call specific agencies and ask, "Who handles new writers?" If you admire an established writer, you may contact the WGA for the name of his or her agent.

The point is to get the names of *individual* agents. You will *not* send them your script. You will instead fax or send a query letter to about five agents at a time. Faxing (or mailing) to five agents at a time enables you to evaluate their responses and improve your query before you contact more agents. You will only contact one agent per agency.

THE QUERY LETTER

The query letter is your key to getting read, and is the professional way to approach agents, producers, executives, talent, and directors. You will fax or mail a concise, one-page query letter to about five agents. Don't get palsy-walsy or cocky with these people. Be professional, but also be creative. This query letter will include the following, not necessarily in order:

1. A story hook (What if the president of the United States was kidnapped?), logline (the *TV Guide* version of the story), or concept (Hard-boiled cop becomes kindergarten teacher). This opening *headline* should *imply* the genre (thriller, action-adventure, etc.) and perhaps state the title. See "How To Pitch Without Striking Out" on page 157 for more on this topic.

2. A brief pitch of the story in terms of character, conflict, and action—beginning, middle, and end. This story summary will be one or two paragraphs, with one being preferred to two. Now, don't tease the agent with a statement like, "If you want to know how it ends, you'll have to read the script." That won't work. However, if your hook is strong enough, you may not need to pitch the entire story. Some writers will begin the letter with the story and omit any kind of hook. The choice is yours, and it is a marketing decision. Just make sure that the first half of your letter makes the agent want to read your script. It's okay to use Hollywood buzzwords and phrases such as "a hero with an edge"—just make sure they're in current usage.

3. Your qualifications. There are many ways to qualify yourself.

- Any film or successful writing experience.

- Expertise in the subject matter. I had a student who had been a rock singer for ten years and her script was about a rock singer. That, I thought, was worth mentioning.

- Winner of a screenwriting contest (or placed).

- Endorsed by a professional. The best endorsements are from professionals who are nonbuyers, such as writers and actors. If a producer, why isn't she buying your script?

- An advanced degree in film or writing, although not as impressive as actual experience.

If you have no qualifications, omit this section. If you live outside the Los Angeles area, consider a statement that you're willing to travel to LA for meetings.

4. Request permission to forward your script. Some writers include a self-addressed, stamped envelope (SASE) or postcard to make it easy for the agent to respond; others abandon this practice as defeatist and add a line in their query that they'll follow-up in a few days. If you fax your query, close with "I'll call in a day or two," since you cannot fax an SASE. When you call, ask the agent or agent's assistant for permission to send them your screenplay.

If an agent or assistant states on the phone that they do not accept unsolicited manuscripts, then ask them for a referral to an agent who does. You could also ask, "May I call back in a few months to see if anything has changed?"

Do not send your script with a query. Do not send a treatment or synopsis to an agent unless requested. You are not selling your story; you are selling your writing skills.

SAMPLE QUERY LETTERS

As mentioned, queries can be used to approach any industry professional. Always query before sending a script. Keep in mind that the purpose of the query is obtain permission to forward the script. You accomplish that by getting the reader excited about your story. Here are a few sample queries.

The Wizard of Oz

```
Dear Ms. Big:

A tornado throws a young farm girl into Oz, a magical land where
she must defeat vengeful witches and sinister flying monkeys to
find her way home. While searching for her way back to Kansas,
Dorothy befriends a cowardly lion, an airhead scarecrow, and a
sentimental, if rusty, tin woodsman.  Each, like Dorothy, feels
outcast and misplaced.

They join forces and journey along a convenient yellow brick road
to ask help from the Wizard of Oz, fighting off the Wicked Witch
of the North along the way; but when they finally destroy the
witch and meet the alleged wizard, they discover that the bless-
ing each traveler seeks has been with them all along.

My latest screenplay, The Wizard of Oz, is a family-oriented
fantasy reminiscent of Star Wars.  Before writing it, I spent a
```

```
month investigating tornados and yellow brick.  I've also written
and produced a community-access cable program about tin woodsmen,
and I've had several short stories published in "Munchkin Daily."
```

```
I'd like to send the complete script of The Wizard of Oz for your
review and possible representation.  An SASE is enclosed for your
reply, or you may call me at 555/555-5555.
```

```
Thank you for considering my work and I'll look forward to hear-
ing from you.
```

```
Sincerely,
```

The above letter was created by screenwriter Joni Sensel for her newsletter. She points out in her commentary that she would address the letter to an individual. In the first paragraph, she identifies the protagonist, her obstacles, and goal. I especially like the last sentence about feeling outcast and misplaced because it identifies an emotion.

The second paragraph tells the agent how Dorothy overcomes her obstacles. It identifies opponents and suggests the resolution. I would omit the word "convenient"—an agent or producer could possibly get the wrong impression that the *journey* is convenient or easy. As you know, the character's journey should be anything but convenient.

The third paragraph refers to STAR WARS. This links the project to a proven success and signals to the agent that *Oz* could be big bucks. (It's usually best to refer to a *current* success.) Joni also indicates the genre and lists her qualifications. She further identifies her research. Although effective here, research efforts aren't normally included.

The fourth and fifth paragraphs tell the agent what to do in a polite way (without groveling). The last paragraph, in my mind, is optional. The reference to an SASE is unnecessary—the SASE will be there for the agent to see. This well-written letter flows smoothly and logically from point to point. If you use the phone to query, be just as succinct and self-assured.

Bed of Lies

This letter is provided by Kerry Cox, editor of the *Hollywood Scriptwriter* newsletter.

```
Dear Ms. Agent:
```

```
Thirteen years ago, J.T. Wheeler woke up at 5:30 a.m., showered, had
a light breakfast, and savagely murdered his family of four. He then
hopped into his Lexus and vanished from the face of the Earth.
```

```
Or did he?
```

It's a question Susan Morgan, wife of prominent attorney Lawrence Morgan, has to answer fast. The chilling fact is, the more she learns, the more she realizes that Wheeler's killing spree not only wasn't his first . . . it may very well not be his last.

And she might be married to him.

BED OF LIES is a psychological thriller and dark mystery with a strong female protagonist, a deeply horrifying villain, and a series of disturbing surprises that builds to an ultimate shocker of an ending. It is also a story of trust, of betrayal, and the fine line that divides the two when secrets are buried between husband and wife.

I'd like to submit BED OF LIES for your consideration and possible representation. I've written professionally for television, radio, and print, including network TV credits and two published books. I've also worked extensively as a crisis-intervention counselor for Interact, a non-profit group specializing in teen and marital crisis management.

I've enclosed a pre-paid postcard for your reply. Thanks very much for your time and consideration.

Sincerely,

Kerry Cox

The first paragraph—with the punchline *Or did he?*—is the hook. The next section is the story, including the title, genre, and underlying theme about trusts and secrets. Next come the qualifications. Kerry's work as a crisis-intervention counselor qualifies him as an expert in the story's subject matter. His writing style matches the mood of the story, and uses detail effectively. If this query was for a comedy, he would probably have written the letter from a humorous slant.

Heart of Silence

What follows is a query letter that won a contest sponsored by the Screenwriter's FORUM. Although the content of the letter is fine, the letter itself needs a shave and a trim. I eliminated words, phrases, and sentences that I felt were unnecessary.

In queries like this, many things are taken for granted. For example, the agent will realize that the writer has completed an original feature film script—why else would she be writing? The strength of this letter, I believe, lies in the intriguing concept hook: *A man [is] forced to confront his own divinity when his dead daughter rescues him from suicide.*

Original

Dear Ms. Pikthis,

I have recently completed an original film script entitled HEART OF SILENCE. It tells the story of a man forced to confront his own divinity when his dead daughter rescues him from suicide. The stage version of this story, entitled CRY OF SILENCE, won the 1989 Kumu Kahua Playwright's Award from the University of Hawaii. The script is 104 pages.

HEART OF SILENCE has been reviewed by a professional reader, Kerry Cox, who commented: "An intelligently written script, professionally written and in proper format. Your characters, particularly the husband, were well-drawn and realistic." Dalene Young, a professional scriptwriter, said the material was "moving, believable, and dramatic."

I have also completed an original feature comedy entitled QUEEN KONG. It is a send-up of KING KONG, in which the hero is the love of the female beast. It runs 110 pages. Both scripts are available upon your request as a hard copy or on disk in WordPerfect 5.1 for IBM.

In addition to works of my own, I am also interested in working on rewrites and collaborations. I am able to travel to take meetings in Los Angeles.

Thank you for your consideration.

Aloha Pumehana,
Karen Mitura

Revised

Dear Ms. Pikthis:

HEART OF SILENCE tells the story of a man forced to confront his own divinity when his dead daughter rescues him from suicide. My stage version of this story won the 1989 Kumu Kahua Playwright's Award from the University of Hawaii.

The screenplay has been reviewed by a professional reader, Kerry Cox, who commented: "An intelligently written script, professionally written . . . Your characters, particularly your husband, were well-drawn and realistic." Dalene Young, a professional screenwriter, said the material was "moving, believable, and dramatic."

Although I have many scripts and story ideas, I am also interested in assignments. I am able to travel to Los Angeles for meetings.

I'll call your office soon. I look forward to speaking to you or your assistant.

Aloha Pumehana,
Karen Mitura

The first paragraph of the revised letter states the title, hints at the genre, pinpoints the concept hook, and affirms one of Karen's qualifications as a writer. The second paragraph continues with two professional endorsements.

In my revision, I omit the reference to QUEEN KONG, but inform the agent that Karen has written other scripts. As a general rule, I believe your query should focus on one screenplay—your best shot—but could mention the fact you have written other scripts.

The third paragraph also shows Karen's flexibility and answers a possible question—is she willing to travel to Los Angeles for meetings? I felt this was a key point in her letter because it shows that she understands the business. She put herself in the agent's shoes and anticipated the agent's question.

The fourth paragraph states that she'll follow-up by phone. If this letter is faxed, the final paragraph would begin, "I'll call your office later today [or tomorrow]."

Did you notice that I did not end with some pleasant expression or statement about wanting representation. I believe the agent knows instinctively that the writer seeks representation. So why state the obvious? I concede that this is a debatable point. Most agents prefer short and sweet letters. The conciseness of Karen's revised letter is worth emulating.

You may have noticed that her letter does not tell the entire story. The thinking here (right or wrong) is that the concept alone is strong enough to elicit a positive response.

The Silk Maze
This final example by Jeff Warshaw capitalizes on Hollywood's penchant for sex. Although a one-paragraph story summary would be preferred to two, notice how Jeff's style creates suspense and intrigue. Jeff presented this in class to a standing ovation.

```
Dear Mr. Shmoe:

Jonathan Stark thought he knew all the angles.  He thought he
knew what Lily, his beloved partner-in-crime, wanted from life.
He thought he knew how to please and manipulate Celia, the young
socialite who seemed to know too much about his sordid past.  He
thought he could control the heart of Mazie, the one "client" who
cared for him.  He was wrong.

Jonathan Stark knew nothing about the three equally beautiful and
treacherous women who ruled his life. Trapped between two women
who love him for very different reasons, and one who wants to
destroy him no matter what it takes, Jonathan must walk the
```

tightrope between the true love he seeks and the easy, swarmy sex
life he's come to know. Will he make the right decision, or is
he riding for the biggest fall of his life? Caught in a smooth,
alluring web of intrigue, deception, and white-hot sexual subter-
fuge, Jonathan Stark must stay one step ahead of the game if he
hopes to escape THE SILK MAZE.

THE SILK MAZE is a fast-paced, erotic thriller with more twists
and turns than a roller coaster as it rockets toward a stunning,
steamy climax. It is the story of a man so used to lies that he
can hardly see the truth before him, a man who must learn to
trust not only his instincts, but himself.

I would like to submit my third script, THE SILK MAZE, for your
consideration and possible representation. I am interested in
rewrites and adaptations. You may call me at (714) 555-5555 at
your convenience.

Very truly yours,

Jeffrey C. Warshaw

Jeff indicates his genre as a fast-paced, erotic thriller. He is wise to give his genre some pizzazz. Erotic thriller is better than thriller. Romantic action/adventure is better than action/adventure. My script KUMQUAT is not a romantic comedy; it is a romantic comedy against the background of high adventure. Don't overdo it, however, with something like sci-fi/action/drama reality-based environmental Western.

Jeff mentions rewrites and adaptations; I would use the broader term "assignments." He concludes his letter with his phone number. Make sure your address and phone number are somewhere on the letter. Don't expect someone to pick it up off your envelope. These days, letterhead is easy to create using virtually any word-processing appplication.

Incidentally, your letterhead need not include anything other than your name, address, and phone number. Don't give yourself the title *screenwriter* or *writer*. It's the sign of an amateur.

Query letters do not need to be long. In evaluating one client's script, I saw a clever angle to her story and wrote a query letter for her. The letter consisted of just one paragraph, and that paragraph was only five lines long. Even though she had no qualifications, she received forty requests for her script. Unfortunately, she had not followed my advice to polish her script before sending the query and to not mass-submit the query. This story, unfortunately, ended in heartbreak.

WHAT NOT TO INCLUDE IN A QUERY LETTER

It can be tough finding the razor's edge between professionalism and creativity. And where does confidence and enthusiasm end and conceit and insolence begin? One rule of thumb is to ask yourself: What does this agent or producer want to hear? In other words, get the focus off you and what you want to say, and get into the head of the agent or producer you're writing to.

Here are excerpts from five would-be screenwriters who didn't figure that out. These were collected by screenwriter Joni Sensel.

> "A warm-hearted, romantic venture into the deepest of human emotions, revolving around the love of one person for another despite overwhelming odds, with a touch of comedy, proving yet again that love conquers all . . . And of course, like all my work, the story concludes with a stunning, unexpected ending."

This could describe a dozen stories. The problem here is the character is telling instead of showing, and is focusing more on theme than story. Write the story, including the ending, and we'll decide if it's heart-warming and stunning.

> "I'm 22. I hope this will be my way over the 'wall' and give me access to a struggling industry that could use the talents I possess to help it reach its potential. Cinema is my life and I hate to see it in the hands of incapable people."

Don't get cocky, kid.

> "Your agency has been highly recommended to me by the Writers Guild. I have enclosed a short story that explains why I have chosen to be a screenwriter."

And we're all dying to read it. And please, no false flattery. Be aware of Linda Buzzell's two no-nos—"don't be dull or desperate" (from *How To Make It In Hollywood*).

> "Jesus Christ the man and I are both empaths. I'm this way because of Y. The symbol of God is a clock. I would like to meet the Pope someday."

Is this the story or your qualifications?

> " . . . the constant epistemological question regarding the perplexing attempt to explain the nature of being and reality and the origins and structure of the world . . . the metaphysical

```
conflict between natural law (St. Augustine) and pragmatism
(Kant-Dewey-James) and the question of the benefits of merging
from . . . "
```

Excuse me, please, but I just wanna make a movie.

ONCE THE QUERY IS SENT

The next step is to evaluate the responses to your query. Half may not respond at all. If you faxed your query letter, call in a couple of days. If you mailed your query, wait a week or so to follow-up.

Usually a phone response is positive. Rejection generally comes through the mail. No response usually means no, although it is possible that the query was lost. If the rejections pile up, then re-evaluate your query and your story. Make any necessary changes. Then go ahead and contact more agents.

Once an agent responds positively to your query, send your script with a cover letter that opens with a variation of, "As you requested, here is . . . " Not much else needs to be said in the cover letter.

The script should be an excellent photocopy of a letter-quality original. Send it priority mail with the cover letter and, if you wish, include return postage. It's okay to make a personal delivery, but you probably will not get a chance to meet the agent.

Wait at least three weeks before following up on a script submission. Try once every week or so after that. Be *pleasantly persistent*. Generally, the best time to call is in the afternoon. A Thursday or Friday call will remind the agent to get the script read over the weekend.

When an agent or assistant says, "We'll call you," or "We'll get back to you," your response will be, "Great! May I call in a week?" That makes it more difficult for them to summarily dismiss you.

If your script has not been read by your third or fourth call, then it's time to blow taps for that agent, but before you do, try to get a referral to another agent. Keep in mind that each agent has about fifteen to twenty clients and is inundated with script submissions, often over 100 a week. Things take time, so be patient. If a script is rejected, try to get some feedback concerning it's weaknesses. Ask for a copy of the coverage.

Always treat the agent's assistant like a human being. Learn his name. Treat him with the same respect you'd accord the agent, and don't use the word "secretary." You may very well need to sell this person first. In fact, it's quite possible that the assistant will be the first and only person to read your script.

No one in Hollywood is an assistant to be an assistant. Everyone is on their way up. So think of the assistant as your friend and accomplice. He can tell you how a particular agency operates. You can ask, for example, "When should I expect to hear from so-and-so?" Or, "When can I call back?" If an agent is too busy to read your work now, you can ask, "May I try back in a few months to see if anything has changed?"

Let me remind you that during this long period of searching for an agent and selling your script, you should not stop writing. Once you finish a script, take a week off and then start another one. Chances are you will finish it before the previous one has been sold.

WORKING WITH YOUR AGENT

When an agent wants to talk to you, she'll call and ask the magic question: "What else have you done?" Hopefully, you have written a second dynamite script, and have other ideas to talk about. There are a few matters that you and your agent will want to take care of before the selling process begins.

One is the contract. The agent gets ten percent. **No reputable agent charges a reading fee.** Be wary of requests for cash or for referrals to specific script consultants. However, an agent may legitimately ask you to cover the cost of photocopying your script.

In Writers Guild-signatory contracts, there is a ninety-day clause. If the agent has not found you work in ninety days, then you can terminate the contract. Before you do, however, remember that selling a script takes time. Many agents will not tender a contract until an offer is made by a producer for your script or services. If your agent is WGA-signatory, then this is usually not a problem—the eventual contract will be WGA-approved.

Your agent will want to discuss your career. What do you want to write? Any genres of particular interest to you? Are you willing to write for television? Are you willing to travel to L.A. for necessary meetings? Are there certain things you are unwilling to write (such as stories that demean women)? Be careful not to sound too picky about what you'll write.

While in Hollywood, choose your battles carefully. Many are not worth fighting; some are.

If you have several scripts, and an agent doesn't like one of them, ask for a release so that you can go out and sell it yourself. If you feel uneasy about a particular agent, ask him to tell you about his current clients and recent sales. You'll get an idea of his ability.

Always remember, the agent's primary motivation is money. Communicate to the agent your desire for a writing career, your willingness to work hard, and to accept writing assignments and development deals. Keep in mind, though, that screenwriters rarely get assignments for adaptations and rewrites unless they've had a big sale.

In addition to commitment, your agent wants to see in you an ability to perform as a writer and as a pitcher—how well you present yourself and your ideas.

In terms of marketing, your agent will suggest a strategy for selling your script. The agent will want to generate heat and interest more than one buyer in your script. This can result in an auction. That's the ideal situation. More likely, however, your agent will use your script as a lure for a meeting or pitching session with a producer in hopes of securing a development deal or other writing assignment.

Some agents get you to work for them. You go out and make the contacts. When someone expresses interest in your script, you say: "I'll have my agent send you a copy."

Stay in touch with your agent. Get together on the phone periodically, or in person. During an active campaign, there should be contact at least once a month.

How to pitch without striking out

What happens when an agent submits your script to a studio or production company? First of all, what is a producer or executive looking for?

To be honest, most have their own ideas to develop if they can just find the right writer. They may also be looking for a writer to do adaptations, or to take over a project where the original writer didn't perform to expectations. Of course, they'll buy a spec script if they think it is an excellent marketing risk, but they're looking for writers. In fact, about eighty-five percent of the deals out there are development deals—producers hiring writers to execute their ideas.

What will your agent do? Well, your agent will contact the highest-level executives and producers he knows. These will be producers with deals or executives at studios. Producers with deals are producers with contracts or other connections with studios or financial sources. The studios are usually the last to be contacted because their rejection closes the doors to outside producers wanting to bring the project to them.

The executive or producer (I'm using the terms synonymously here) will normally give the script to a *story editor*, who will assign it to a *story analyst* or *reader*. The reader, as stated before, writes a *coverage* and makes a recommendation. If the recommendation is positive, the development executive will read at least a portion of your screenplay.

A development executive must love your script to champion it. Assuming he does love it, he will present it to other execs, who will read it over the weekend. It will then be discussed at the Monday morning conference. The decision will be made to buy it or not.

If they decide to buy it, you could be rolling in six figures. If they decide to pass on the script, but they like the writing, the executive will call your agent and ask to meet you. This means you're a semi-finalist in your bid to secure a development deal or other writing assignment. Your agent will arrange a meeting.

THE MEETING

Just a few years ago, *the meeting* was a forum for writers to pitch their ideas. Often, the producer would choose one of the ideas and hire the writer to write the script—a development deal. These days, that first meeting works something like this:

You'll be seated on a soft couch or conference table facing two or more executives. They know in advance that you are nervous. They will be kind and courteous, so try to relax. Dress comfortably enough to feel at ease and professionally enough to convey your respect for those in attendance. Place your hind quarters hard against the back of the chair or couch—this helps you project your voice and maintain good posture.

Be yourself, if at all possible. Project positive energy—not Pollyanna, not God's gift to Hollywood—but upbeat and confident. You will speak with the voice of conviction about your work. But first get the conversation going. Ask about something in the office—a trophy or painting.

The producers want to get a feeling that they can work with you and that you have creative ideas. They may ask you what you're working on and you may have a chance to briefly pitch one or more ideas. This brief pitch may be similar to how you'd present your story in a query letter. The following pointers will also help.

THE TWO-MINUTE PITCH

Brief pitches come in two stages—the headline in twenty-five words or less, and a brief rendition of the storyline.

The headline must grab their attention and set a tone. The headline could be the story hook, the premise, the logline, or the concept. (See "The low down on high concept" in Book I, pages 16-18.) Here are examples of headlines.

- *Honey, I Shrunk the Kids. Family comedy.* Here you've identified the title and genre.

- *Family/sci-fi/thriller. An alien child accidentally left behind on Earth is befriended by some children who help him find his way home.* This is the logline for E.T.

- *JAWS in space.* This is the headline used to pitch ALIEN.

- *The Secret of Question Mark Cave is the story of a secret cave, a magic sword, and a family stranded without a TV set.* This story hook implies the genre.

- *What if the President of the United States were kidnapped?* This is a premise statement.

- *Romance against a background of high adventure: When her sister is kidnapped, a lonely romance writer tries to save her, only to find true romance in the process.* This is a variation of the old pitching formula: When X happens (the Big Event), so-and-so tries to get Y, but ends up with Z.

- *Imagine you are driving down a dark road. Late at night. And someone is behind you. You turn; he turns. He is following you. You decide to get on a lighted street and suddenly find yourself at a stop light. No where to go and the car behind you gets closer and closer. Finally, he pulls up next to you and stops. You look over and he resembles you exactly. He is you!* This is a little long, but it's an example of a story hook.

Remember, concept is what sells: *What if Peter Pan grew up?* On the other hand, if the producer's past work consists of character-driven material, a high-concept pitch may not be appropriate; in fact, you may even be perceived as a hack. Be wise.

Once you have awed them with your headline, you will be favored with a nod or otherwise be encouraged to continue. You will then deliver your two-minute storyline. Present the entire story—beginning, middle, and end—building on what you've already told them. Your focus will be on two or three characters, conflict, emotion, and action. Don't forget the Big Event, the Crisis, and Showdown.

You may pitch anywhere from two to eight ideas, depending on the meeting and the producers. Don't try to pitch too many ideas at once. Your agent will prep you. Keep in mind that the main purpose of this Chamber of Horrors is to provide them a means of evaluating you and your work. Do you have good ideas? Can they work with you?

THE LONG PITCH

When the pitching is over, the producers may share with you an idea or two that they're thinking about. For example, a producer may say, "We're looking for a Faustian comedy for Jimmy Megastar. What do you think?"

If you respond positively and intelligently, the executive may say, "Well, if you come up with a story for us, then let us know. We'd love to hear the pitch." Interpreted this means: Congratulations, you are now a finalist in your bid to secure a development deal. Have your agent call us when you have a ten- to twenty-minute pitch ready.

Here's what's really happening: You and a dozen other finalists will create and pitch a Faustian Comedy for Jimmy Megastar. This way, the producer can develop her ideas without investing a dime of her own money. The producer will pick the pitch she likes best, and you will get the development deal to write the script.

Obviously, you will want to prepare for this major pitch, or for any pitch. Here's how.

Do not read your pitch, but it's okay to have 3" x 5" cards or notes to prompt you. You will be as clear and animated as your personality allows—be your best self. You'll open with your headline followed by the storyline. You may also wish to introduce your key characters right at the beginning before you move into your story.

In the body of the pitch, focus on character, the goal, what's at stake, the emotional high points, how the character will grow, the major dramatic twists, and, of course, how it ends. Two common traps to avoid:

> First, don't try to cram your entire story and all the characters into your pitch. It shouldn't sound too complicated.

Second, don't present a run-down of scenes: *This happens and then this happens and then this happens . . .* Your story will sink into the mud and you'll be dead in the water. Get to the heart. Talk them through the story.

Here's the opening of a successful pitch I delivered for THE SECRET OF QUESTION MARK CAVE. I had just delivered the headline.

My story is about a boy, Seebee, who feels that his dad hates him. He does everything he can to please his dad, but Frankie berates him, criticizes him, hurts him. It's not that Frankie hates his son—he doesn't. He just wishes he knew how to show his affection.

Well, one night, Seebee sneaks into the attic against Frankie's orders and finds the old journal of his great, great grandfather. The journal tells the boy about a secret cave and a magic sword. Wow—with a sword like that, Seebee could solve all his problems! He vows to run away to the mountains, but then he hears a noise! Frankie is downstairs, and boy is he mad.

Of course, your pitch will continue all the way to the end of the story. Please note that in bringing you to the story Catalyst, I emphasized the *emotions* of the characters. The pitch needs to touch the executive's cold heart.

Another angle I could have taken with this pitch would have been to associate a character with a particular actor who could act the role; for example: "See Elijah Wood here." Why do this? To make it easy for the producer to instantly visualize the character. This is the only situation where you should try this device.

In some pitches, you may be interrupted with questions, requests for clarifications, and suggestions. Go with the flow and be flexible, but do not allow the pitch to lose momentum. Be open to suggestions and be prepared to present a different angle on the story.

When they are done with you, they will excuse you. Their decision will be conveyed to your agent. Regardless of the outcome, send a note of thanks.

Be enthusiastic

Remember that one key to successful pitching is the enthusiasm in your voice and the belief you have in your project. You must speak with the voice of conviction. You must believe and make them believe. After all, you are asking them to ultimately invest millions in your story. Enthusiasm is contagious. If you don't feel passion for your story, they will certainly not feel secure about investing in it.

Be creative

In preparing for a long pitch, consider a creative approach. One client used action figures to represent his characters. He introduced them one-by-one and spread them out on the table. The development executive was enthralled. A student pitched his fantasy story in standing position while waving an antique "magic" wand. Another student casually tossed the morning newspaper on the table to draw attention to the issue her story would dramatize. I've even heard stories of writers hiring actors to perform the pitch for them. Don't be afraid to use your voice for emphasis. A minor innovation like that may make your pitch stand out from the dozens of hum-drum presentations that have dulled the producer's senses that week.

Be prepared

The single best way to prepare for a pitch is to invite some friends and neighbors over and pitch to them. If the story appears clear and interesting to them, then feel encouraged. Practicing your pitch in front of real people will help you immensely in preparing for the real thing. You might even role play the entire meeting from beginning to end.

You may be wondering, Why can't I just give producers a synopsis of the story in writing? Why do I have to pitch it? Because they cannot "legally" ask for anything in writing without paying you for it. That's because they are signatory to the Writers Guild of America. However, many writers leave a synopsis or treatment on the table after their pitch. If you're dealing with a producer who is not signatory to the Guild, then you can give him a synopsis or treatment directly and avoid pitching altogether. This is discussed in depth in the next section.

If your pitch does the trick, you will be offered a development deal. Your first development deal could be $50,000-70,000. It will probably also be a step deal, which means you can be cut out at any step in the writing process. You'll be paid a portion of the total purchase price at each step. Although there are many possibilities, it could work like this: 25% advance, 25% on treatment (first step), 25% on first draft (second step), 25% on polish (third step). If the film is eventually produced, expect another $50,000-100,000 production bonus.

Throughout the writing process, you will receive notes from producers or executives-in-charge, and will experience first hand what has come to be known as story *development hell*. This refers to the process of working with the notes and other feedback you'll recieve while developing the project. You may be amazed at how these professionals view your script. Be open to criticism, but be diplomatic and firm where it matters. Your agent will guide you through this gauntlet.

How to sell your script without an agent

Would you be surprised if I told you that many first scripts are sold without an agent? It's true. And although it's a distinct advantage to have an agent, it's possible for you to sell your script without one.

If you decide to sell the script yourself, you will have to research and hustle. However, you will make contacts along the way. Remember, every contact is an important one, so nurture every one you make. The producer who rejected your script but liked it enough to ask about your next project is a golden contact. Stay in touch with an occasional note or call keeping him apprised of your progress.

TEN MARKETING TOOLS

Before you try to sell you script on your own, you need a complete set of marketing tools. Assemble these *before* making your move.

1. A showcase script
You need a great script (preferably two or more) that is proof of your writing ability and can be used as a calling card. If you want to break into television, you will need one feature script and at least one sample television script.

2. A pitch headline
As mentioned, this will consist of a logline, one-sentence concept hook, or premise statement that you can insert into a query letter, use over the phone, or pitch in person.

3. A brief story summary
This will be one or two paragraphs in length and can be used in your query or as part of your pitch. This, along with your pitch headline, comprise the two-minute pitch.

4. A one-page synopsis

This can be attached to a query letter (directed to producers or talent) or delivered in a pitch. In fact, a synopsis is a written pitch, and many producers will want to see a synopsis before reading the script.

5. A treatment (sometimes called *outline*)

This is not the long, fifty-page treatment that you're paid to write in a development deal. This *spec* treatment is three to seven pages—three pages are usually better than seven. (Don't confuse this *outline* with the more detailed scene-by-scene *step outline*.)

A treatment is actually a long synopsis—a written pitch, analogous to the long pitch discussed earlier—double-spaced and written in present-tense narrative form with no or little dialogue. It's not a scene-by-scene rundown, and you will only focus on about three or four characters. It emphasizes the crucial moments, the key events of the story, and the emotional highs and lows of your characters. This treatment not only tells the story, but it sells the story. It is a marketing piece. You write it for producers, talent, and directors—you want them to love the story. You want them to say, "What a great concept! Let me read the script!"

Don't expect to find work based on a treatment alone until you are established. You must have a finished script. If a producer loves your treatment, your story, but you have no script, he will buy the story for $1,000 (if you're lucky) and then hire a proven writer to write the script. Hollywood has plenty of ideas, but few great writers. Great ideas are not worth much without a script.

Both a treatment and a synopsis can be registered with the Writers Guild. Follow the same process as registering a screenplay.

6. A hot, one-page query letter for every occasion

Never send a script to anyone cold. Always query first. Even if you are responding to an ad asking for a script, you should query first.

Your pithy, professional query will creatively present your concept, along with the title and the genre, which may be implied rather than directly stated. It will then convey your complete story in a paragraph or two, or will simply refer to the attached synopsis. Your query will then list your qualifications and ask permission to send your script on spec. Approach no more than ten producers at a time.

If you know in advance how a particular producer or actor likes to be queried, then those instructions supersede my own.

7. A telephone script

You need this next to your phone when you call anyone about your screenplay or teleplay, or they call you. Don't be like a student of mine who was called back on a query and who blanked out on the phone. After six seconds of silence, the agent hung up. Quickly, she called me and I told her to call the agent immediately and explain that she had a cold and had lapsed into a coughing spell. Fortunately, her explanation was satisfactory.

The key element of your telephone script is your two-minute pitch (#2 and #3 above). You will carry a copy wherever you go. It's better to improvise off notes than to read. Also, prepare pitches of other scripts you've written or want to write and have them handy. This is in case you're asked the golden question: "What else have you done?"

A telephone script is what all professional telemarketers use. It tells you what to say if the person on the other line says yes, no, or makes a particular excuse or objection. Here's just one possible example:

> "I'm [name]. I'm a screenwriter with a [name genre, such as action/romantic comedy] that I think might be right down your alley. May I send it to you?"

> (What's it about?) [Here you will pitch it, leading with a headline, logline, premise, or concept; then, if you feel encouraged, moving into the story summary.]

> (I'm sorry, we're developing our own projects.) "Great. Would you like to read this with an eye toward a possible assignment? I'd love to hear what you're doing [or] I loved NAZIS IN SPACE [or whatever his/her last production was]. [Here you are identifying your script as a mere sample of your work. You hope it will lead to a meeting and a writing assignment. You're not looking to sell the script itself.]

> (Do you have an agent?) "Actually, I'm making a decision between several agents, so I'm shopping the script now rather than letting it gather dust." [Or] "I'm looking right now. If you have any suggestions, I'd be delighted to hear them."

> (We can't accept a script without an agent.) "Why don't I send it with a release?" [The release is a legal document discussed at the bottom of page 167.]

(I'm sorry, we're not interested.) "Fine. Tell me, is there someone you know who might be interested in this material?" [You might just get a referral here.]

Keep in mind that you may need to "sell" the assistant first before reaching the party you want. Be professional with all parties that you deal with.

8. A list of resources
You have that, you lucky pup! Check Book V. Review these carefully and consider how you can use these resources.

As to the publications, I would start with the following: *Script* published by the Screenwriter's FORUM, the *Hollywood Scriptwriter*, and *Premiere*. *Premiere* will give you a good feel for what is happening in the business. You can subscribe to the "trades" (*Variety*, *Hollywood Reporter*) later. As to the directories, I recommend *The Hollywood Creative Directory*.

9. An inventory of your strengths and the strengths of your script
You will intimate these by how you present yourself and your work.

10. A list of referrals, and the individual names of producers, directors, and talent
First, as stated before, list all the people you know who are in the business and all the people you know who might know someone in the business. Then make lists of individual producers, directors, and talent who might be interested in your work. The names can be had from the many directories around. There are directories of large producers and independent producers, including talent and directors with their own production companies. These directories are listed in Book V.

As to producers, actors, and directors, you may wish to choose those who have worked on projects similar to your own. Their names can be found on the films they have made. Also, check out the "Film and TV Production Charts" in the trades as to what is currently in production.

Every February, independent producers, foreign sales agents, and others gather for the American Film Market (AFM). A directory is printed by both the AFM and the *Hollywood Reporter*. In addition, keep a lookout in the trades, screenwriting publications, and directories.

The key is to get lists of the individual names of people who might be interested in your work. Always write to people, not to companies.

APPROACHING YOUR MARKET

Now that you have these ten tools in your toolbox, you can mastermind your campaign. Don't be overly concerned with Hollywood trends. Who can tell what they will be? What they want now may not be what they'll be looking for a year from now. As a general rule, however, you can expect an interest in action/adventure scripts, thrillers, good comedies, and "date" movies for couples.

More importantly, make sure your screenplay is original, and don't write a script that will cost $100 million to produce, particularly if you are approaching the indies who make low-budget features in the $500 thousand to $2 million range.

Keep in mind that your first script usually becomes a sample script that you use as a calling card. That's why my advice is to write what you have a passion for. You need that energy to get you through that first script.

There are five groups of people you can approach to sell your script without an agent:

1. Writers Guild-signatory producers
2. Independent producers (the indies)
3. Actors and directors
4. Network television producers
5. Cable, independent television, regional markets, and the new technologies—Hollywood's back door

Writers Guild-signatory producers

The studios and other large production companies are signatory to the Guild. They have agreed to use Writers Guild-approved contracts. Their names can be easily found in a variety of directories.

The large producers have deals with studios, meaning they have contractual arrangements to produce a certain number of pictures with a studio or production company, or a studio may have right of first refusal. This is one reason it is better to let a producer take your project to a studio than to go directly to the studio yourself. These producers are big because they have access to the money needed to finance a picture. Generally, they accept submissions only from agents.

However, if your query is strong enough, there are some WGA-signatory producers who may accept a script without an agent. In such cases, they will require a *submission agreement* or *release*. A submission agreement is a legal document that basically absolves the producer or executive of responsibility if your work is accidentally stolen. It sounds horrible, but you should consider signing the release to get your work sold and produced.

Generally, these folks aren't interested in stealing your story. Theft occurs occasionally, but large producers and studios are more interested in avoiding lawsuits than they are in theft. *Writer's paranoia* is the hallmark of an amateur. You've got to get your ideas out there. Perhaps your best protection is your writing ability and industry savvy.

The indies

If you are taken to the cleaners, it will more likely be by an independent producer. Most of these are not signatory to the Guild, so there are fewer restraints keeping these guys off the paths of temptation. You need to be aware of this because your first sale may be to an independent producer.

Be professional in contacting independent producers, beginning with a query letter plus your synopsis or a phone call. They seldom require submissions through agents, but may ask you to sign a release.

The indies are notoriously cheap. It's not uncommon to have your pay deferred, or to be paid just a few thousand dollars. Seldom are you paid anything up front. In fact, they normally offer a *literary purchase and option agreement*, commonly called *option*. They will pay you a small amount of money, say $500, to tie up the rights to your script for a period of time, say six months. If the agreed-upon purchase price is $10,000, the producer must pay that amount before the six-month deadline. If he does, the producer owns the script. If he doesn't, the rights revert back to you, plus you keep the $500.

With an option, a producer can tie up the rights with just a few dollars. In fact, it is not unusual for an indie to ask for a "free" option—no money down. During the option period, the producer uses your script to attract talent, a director, or some other element. Once he has a *package*, he goes to the money people and shops for a deal. If a deal is secured, he pays you for the script.

Even if you're paid very little for your first assignment, a sale is a sale. You can begin building your career on such a sale. And credits, at this point, are worth more to your career than money. On the other hand, I had one student who sold his first script to an independent producer in New York for $110,000. So there is a wide variety of opportunities in these markets.

Don't be tempted to sign a deal that's bad for you. Don't write until you have a completed deal. And if you're not being paid as stipulated, then stop writing.

If a contract is slow in coming, request a deal memo. A deal memo is a quicky contract that presages the larger edition later on. It can be used to cinch a deal, any kind of deal.

The producer may say, "I'll have my assistant send you a deal memo until we draw up the contracts." The deal memo is simply a letter delineating the basic points of the deal. Sign the letter and return it. Some time later, the actual contract will arrive.

A great number of independent producers are searching for scripts for very low-budget productions ($100,000 to $500,000 and up) with as few as one or two locations and just a handful of characters. This market should not be overlooked.

Actors and directors

Don't approach actors and directors through their agents, because their agents will not see you as potential money and will not pass the script along. The best way to approach these people is to make a personal delivery. This is easier said than done. One writer found an actress in a public place and fell to his knees. With his script in hand, he gushed obsequiously, "I adore you. You have such range. Here, I wrote this for you and for you alone. Please, would you read it?" She did.

Many actors and directors have their own production companies, which are set up specifically to find projects equal to their talents. Most require script submissions through agents. Some will accept a script with a release.

When there's a will, there's a way

Sometimes you need a creative way to bring attention to your script. For example, dress up as a custodian after hours and drop the script on someone's desk. A friend of mine dressed up as a UPS man and delivered his script to Harrison Ford. Harrison Ford actually signed for it. Too bad the script was such a dog. Another writer sent his script in a pizza box. CAUTION: Don't be so clever that you offend the talented person.

THE TICKING MAN was sold by an agent who sent alarm clocks to about twenty producers. A note said, "The ticking man is coming." This resulted in a bidding war and the script sold for $1 million.

After graduating from my class, Robert Olague imprinted the logline for his screenplay THE COMING on the back of a jacket, and attended a writers' conference. The logline read, *In an attempt to take over the world, an alien imitates the coming of a messiah*. Robert made many key contacts that night.

There are almost as many ways to break into the business as there are writers. Just remember, before you parachute into Michelle Pfeiffer's backyard, be sure you are carrying with you a great script. Don't leave home without it.

Television and Hollywood's back door

There are many opportunities in television. And television is where the money and power is for writers, but network television is hard to break into. Television is concept-driven, and most of it is staff written. That's because they want to use proven talent. In most cases, you will need an agent to break into the networks. You may ask: Well then, how do I break into television?

First, write a showcase feature script that you can use as a sample. It's the best way to enter any movie or TV market. It shows you can create characters and a cogent story from scratch.

Movie-of-the-Week (MOW)

The MOW market is tough to break into at the network level. Disease of the Week and period dramas are particularly tough for the newcomer to sell. Approach MOW producers as you would WGA-signatory movie producers. As mentioned earlier, the easiest way to break into this market is through ownership of rights to a true story. Keep in mind that your network MOW audience is composed primarily of middle-aged women.

The back door into this area is through non-network MOW producers. For the first time in history (1994), less than fifty percent of TV movies are being developed and produced for network television. This is good news for you because most of these non-network markets—such as pay TV, Turner, and other cable stations—are, at the moment, open to new writers, and you may not need an agent to enter many of them. Audience demographics vary from outlet to outlet.

Pilots

If you have never sold a script and want to develop a pilot or miniseries, you might as well try parting the Red Sea. Generally, you need a track record as a TV writer before you're granted entrance into this arena. Your best strategy is to write your TV pilot as a movie script. Then in the selling process, as people express interest, you can say, "You know, it'd make a great TV show."

Episodic television

To break into episodic television, and situation comedy in particular, you write a feature-length script plus one or two TV scripts similar to the show you want to write for. These are submitted as work samples. Generally, if you want to write for SEINFELD, you don't submit a SEINFELD script. The errors in your script will be very obvious to the story editor of that series. They tend to look at scripts for their own shows with a jaundiced eye. Instead, submit a FRASIER script or a script for some other sitcom.

Before you write a TV episodic script, ask the producer for the show's bible. The bible is a printed guide that sets forth the rules of the show, including character sketches, and information on what's forbidden and what they're looking for. The STAR TREK bible even delineates what can and cannot be done on the Enterprise, and includes detailed drawings of the ship. Some producers may not send you a bible except through an agent.

Now write a couple of scripts and submit one or more to the TV producer of your choice. The WGA *Journal* lists TV markets that are open. If the producer or executive likes your work sample, then a meeting will be arranged. This meeting is a forum set up for you specifically to pitch story ideas for episodes. Have a dozen ready to go. If you've reached this milestone, it means you are being considered to write one or more episodes.

In pitching, use the same guidelines presented earlier. The opening headline for your SEINFELD script could be, "Kramer goes berserk and holds Seinfeld hostage." Keep in mind that producers often make up their minds in the first thirty seconds of the pitch.

The back door

Perhaps the best way to break into the writing business is through Hollywood's back door. It's not as closely guarded and fewer writers are trying this entrance. There is a huge market in public, independent, pay, and cable television. Think of all the stations and networks that must provide programming twenty-four hours a day: HBO, Showtime, Vestron, Lorimar, Turner Broadcasting, the super stations, and the dozens of new cable networks, stations, and channels.

The PBS network includes such stalwarts as KCET in Los Angeles, WNET in New York, WGBH in Boston, and ETV in South Carolina. Approach these stations individually or PBS directly. Don't overlook the American Playhouse and Wonderworks consortia.

One evening after presenting a seminar on the East Coast, I received a call from a very young eighteen-year-old who had never written so much as a page. He told me he had called a PBS station and presented a series idea over the phone. The producer loved it, but since the kid did not have a sample script, the producer suggested he connect with a professional writer. Imagine! If this kid had had a decent sample script (or had been willing to write one), he likely would have been hired.

DTV (Direct-To-Video) provides opportunities for many writers. These are low-budget ($1-1.5 million) made-for-video videos (mostly action/adventure and thrillers) that are never released theatrically. Approach independent producers for these.

Related to this area is the information/instructive video market. Videos such as *Buns of Steel* and *How to Remodel Your Home* are examples. Keep in mind that regardless of the market, the basic approach is similar in each.

Already mentioned are the non-network TV movie markets (page 170) and the many low-budget producers looking for scripts that can be produced for less than a half million (page 169), $1-2 million, and so on. Also note the regional markets (page 174).

Don't ignore the many magazine shows, educational shows, soap operas, animated shows, children's shows, game shows, infomercials (Direct Response Television), and reality programming. Since scripts for animated feature-length movies earn about half as much as regular features, this becomes an area of less competition and perhaps more opportunity for beginning writers. And keep an eye at how the coming *electronic film distribution system* alters the marketplace.

Interactive programming
Video games, videos based on video games, interactive programming, multimedia, and CD-ROM represent markets on the rise. In fact, I believe this broad area will become a huge growth industry with increasing opportunities for writers. In fact, production has increased markedly in the first quarter of 1995.

At the moment, producers in this area are open to ideas. Surprisingly, it is better to approach these people with a treatment than with a completed script—at least for now. Also include game concepts and flow charts if applicable. Your final script may earn you $25,000 to $50,000.

Keep in mind that this market is growing rapidly and the parameters may change rapidly as well. There are many interactive companies now. Most studios and many special-effects companies have formed interactive divisions. Contact them directly or have your agent call.

Videos for business and education

More money is spent in non-broadcast audio-visual than in the U.S. motion picture and television industry. Kodak sells more raw stock to Detroit than to Hollywood. Writing videos for business and education can be both profitable and fun.

You will contact video producers (see the yellow pages) for possible assignments, or call video production managers at corporations. Present yourself as a freelance writer and have a sample twelve-page script handy. In some instances, your other writing experience may be sufficient.

Pay is about $150 per finished minute of the eventual video, or ten percent of budget. That comes to about $1,500 a week for your time.

Knock and the door shall open

The truth is, writing opportunities are springing up everywhere. Overall, the pay is generally lower at the back door, but the experience is good. Use these markets as a platform to greater success.

How to break into Hollywood when you live in Peoria

Living outside of the Los Angeles area is only a problem *after* you've sold your first script and *only* if you're selling directly to a Hollywood-based company. And it may not be a problem even then. You can market your first script from anywhere.

Most Hollywood producers are more concerned about your writing ability than your current domicile. If you write well and seem to know what you're talking about, their fears will be allayed. However, here is what an L.A.-based agent will want to know:

- Are you willing to visit Los Angeles on occasion to attend meetings with producers and executives?

• If a deal is struck, are you willing to relocate to the Los Angeles area?

Here, you will prevaricate. Obviously, if the deal is sweet enough, you will relocate. But don't worry, it won't be forever. Once you have established your name, you can buy a farm in Vermont and write there.

If you want to write for episodic television, you must live near production headquarters, but don't move until you get the assignment.

You'll be pleased to know that more regional opportunities are opening up all the time. There are four reasons for this. Hollywood and Los Angeles are in decline—in some respects, they resemble the fall of the Roman Empire. Union shoots in Southern California have become very expensive. California is generally unfriendly to business. And the Information Age has created a huge demand for programming.

Review the previous section and note how many new opportunities exist in areas outside of Hollywood. Production companies are sprouting up all over the map. Some of these can be found in industry periodicals, directories, or literary references guides. Call around. Your state film commissioner should have up-to-date information concerning the film industry in your state.

Although there are agencies in every part of this country, you may not need an agent to sell to the many independent, regional markets. Look for opportunities in your own backyard; you may be surprised at the acres of diamonds you find there.

In summary, don't let your current residence deter you from pursuing a screenwriting career. Concentrate on your writing first and your geographical problems second.

A personal challenge

Now just a few words concerning your writing career. Take it seriously. You are a screenwriter.

Have a writing schedule. Four hours a day is ideal, but if that is unfeasible, try to set aside whatever time you can. That's your time to write. Your loved ones need to understand that.

Keep logs of contacts, power lunches, phone calls, script submissions, queries, and anything that would affect the "business" of your career. You need this information for follow-ups. This business is built on contacts and relationships. Even when your script is rejected, if anything positive takes place between you and the contact, nurture that contact with occasional notes (once or twice a year) or calls. In doing this, do not impose on their time. And hold on to your screenplay—it may be the perfect vehicle ten years hence.

Keep track of your expenses. I'm afraid the IRS will insist on it. You will use the Schedule C to report income and business expenses. You must make a profit in three of the first five years that you declare yourself to be a writer. IRS Booklet 334 would be helpful if it were easier to understand.

If you have a writing partner, be sure to have an agreement before you write, especially if he or she is your best friend. It should cover these points.

- The time each will contribute
- Who gets top writing credit
- What happens if someone drops out or doesn't perform

Keep a writer's notebook of thoughts, ideas, clippings, bits of dialogue, etc. Some writers carry small microcassette recorders. Treat your writing career with respect.

Continue your education, but don't stop writing to learn.

Learn how to take criticism. Be able to stand apart from your work and look at it objectively. Don't rush into rewrites; let advice sink in. Consider what others suggest, but remember that you are the screenwriter and the script is yours until it is sold.

Most of all, enjoy writing for the sake of writing, whether you sell anything or not. Creating something new and original is its own reward. Writing is a fundamentally worthwhile way to spend your time. It's good therapy, too. If you write because you want to, then the financial rewards are more likely to follow.

Writers write.

Now, finally, I'd like to take a moment to salute you. You have not chosen an easy road. You will need to draw upon your inner resources and believe in yourself. When you get up in the morning, face the person in the mirror and say, "I am the next great screenwriter." Then perhaps one morning, you may awaken to find that you are the next great screenwriter. Don't be surprised. Just keep writing.

RESOURCES

AND

INDEX

Resources

INDUSTRY ORGANIZATIONS AND GUILDS

Academy of Motion Picture Arts and Sciences, 8949 Wilshire Blvd., Beverly Hills, CA 90211. (310) 247-3000. Script library.

Academy of Television Arts and Sciences, 3500 W. Olive Ave., Burbank, CA 91505. (818) 953-7575. Script library.

American Film Market Association, 12424 Wilshire Blvd., Suite 600, Los Angeles, CA 90025. (310) 447-1555. Operates annual February independent film market in Santa Monica.

Directors Guild of America, 7920 Sunset Blvd., Los Angeles, CA 90046. (310) 289-2000. In New York: 110 W. 57th St., New York, NY 10019. (212) 581-0370. Sells a directory of members.

National Creative Registry, 1106 Second St., Encinitas, CA 92024. 1-800-DU-U-WRITe. Provides a script registration service for less than the WGA.

Producers Guild of America, 400 S. Beverly Dr., #211, Beverly Hills, CA 90212. (310) 557-0807.

Screen Actors Guild, 5757 Wilshire Blvd., Los Angeles, CA 90036. (213) 954-1600. In New York: 1515 Broadway, 44th Floor, New York, NY 10036. (212) 944-1030. Call for the phone number of a specific actor's agency or point-of-contact.

Women in Film, 6464 Sunset Blvd., #530, Los Angeles, CA 90028. (213) 463-6040. Provides a variety of services and programs to foster professional growth. To join, you must have at least one year of professional or academic experience.

Writers Guild of America, east, Inc., 555 W. 57th St., New York, NY 10019. (212) 767-7800. Registration Service is $22; Agency List is available for a nominal charge. Sells a directory of agents and members. Services available to non-members.

Writers Guild of America, west, Inc., 8955 Beverly Blvd., Los Angeles, CA 90048-2456. (310) 550-1000. Direct Dial: (310) 205-2541. Agency list—Nominal charge. Script library. WGA Registration Service—$20.00 (9009 Beverly Blvd.). Open 10-noon, 2-5, Monday-Friday (310) 205-2500. Services available to non-members.

SEMINARS, SCHOOLS, SCRIPT ANALYSIS AND CONSULTANTS, AND OTHER SERVICES

Adams, Jack, 22931 Sycamore Creek Dr., Valencia, CA 91354, (805) 297-2000. Seminars and script consulting for film and television.

American Film Institute, 2021 N. Western Ave., Los Angeles, CA 90027. (213) 856-7690, 1-800-999-4AFI. In New York: 1180 Avenue of the Americas, 10th Floor, New York, NY 10036. (212) 398-6890. Seminars and courses.

Bales, Gail, 5368 E. Willowick, Anaheim, CA 92807. (714) 998-5614. Researcher.

California Community Foundation, 606 S. Olive St., Suite 2400, Los Angeles, CA 90014-1526. (213) 413-4042. Library; reference source for foundations and grants.

Columbia College, 925 N. LaBrea Ave., Hollywood, CA 90038.

Cyberspace Film School. Hollywood Film Institute's Global Film School is on the web. http://www.hollywoodu.com/hifi/. (213) 933-3456.

DiMaggio, Madeline, P.O. Box 1172, Pebble Beach, CA 93953. (408) 373-7776. TV script analysis and seminars.

Grant, Ms. Lou, P.O. Box 10277, Burbank, CA 91510-0277. (818) 842-3912. Script consultant.

Hilltop Productions (Michael Hauge), P.O. Box 55728, Sherman Oaks, CA 91413. (818) 995-8118. Script analysis and seminars.

Hollywood Film Institute (Dov S-S Simens), 5225 Wilshire Blvd., Suite 410, Los Angeles, CA 90036. 1-800-366-3456. Two-day film-school crash course. Producing, writing, directing, and financing classes. Cyberspacc Film School. Audio tapes and books.

Hollywood Ink, 7537 Kimdale Lane, Hollywood, CA 90046. Script consulting.

Hollywood Scriptwriting Institute, 1605 N. Cahuenga Blvd., Suite 211, Hollywood, CA 90028. (213) 461-8333. Home study.

Internet Entertainment Network. Homepage: http://HollywoodNetwork.com. E-mail: toHollywood@HollywoodNetwork.com. (310) 288-1881.

Leder, Rich, 15023 Dickens St., #10, Sherman Oaks, CA 91403. (818) 981-0136. Script consultant.

Literary & Screenplay Consultants, 22647 Ventura Blvd., Suite 524, Woodland Hills, CA 91364. (818) 887-6554. Script analysis.

Los Angeles Community Access Library Line. 1-800-312-6641. You may call to verify facts of science, history, etc.

New York Film Academy, 100 E. 17th St., New York, NY 10003. (212) 674-4300. Total immersion, eight-week workshops where each individual writes, directs, shoots, and edits his of her own film.

New York University, Tisch School of the Arts, 721 Broadway, New York, NY 10003. (212) 998-1820.

Paonessa, Leslie, 2231 Montana Ave., #3, Santa Monica, CA 90403. (310) 395-3648. Story analyst/reader. Coverage and story analysis: $75-125.

Rosenberg, Ms. Lynn, 8306 Wilshire Blvd., Suite 249, Beverly Hills, CA 90211. (310) 285-0100. Research consultant.

Screenwriters Incorporated (Syd Field), 270 N. Canon Dr., #1355, Beverly Hills, CA 90210. (310) 271-7975. Seminars and script analysis.

Screenwriting Center (Dave Trottier), 869 East 4500 South, #100, Salt Lake City, UT 84107. (801) 288-4150. Message line: (800) 264-4900. Correspondence course, script and story evaluation, writers' groups, seminars, workshops, retreats, query evaluation, books, and information.

Seger, Dr. Linda, 2038 Louella, Venice, CA 90291. (310) 390-1951. Script doctor and script consultant. Highly recommended.

Simon, Danny, 15233 Magnolia Blvd., #302, Sherman Oaks, CA 91403. Eight-week comedy-writing course.

Storytech (Christopher Vogler), 941 Amoroso Place, Venice, CA 90291. (310) 822-1587. Script consulting and seminars.

Stuart, Linda, (310) 824-0591. Story analyst/author/script consultant. Has taught at AFI.

Truby's Writers Studio, 1739 Midvale Ave., Los Angeles, CA 90024. (310) 575-3050. 1-800-33-TRUBY. Seminars, script consulting, and contest for students.

Two Arts, Inc. (Robert McKee), 12021 Wilshire Blvd., Suite 868, Los Angeles, CA 90025. (310) 312-1002. Seminars, script analysis.

UCLA, Dept of Film and Television, 405 Hilgard Ave., Los Angeles, CA 90024.

USC, School of Cinema-Television, University Park, Los Angeles, CA 90089.

Voluntary Lawyers for the Arts, 1 E. 53rd St., 6th Floor, New York, NY 10022. (212) 319-2910. Provides free arts-related legal assistance to low-income artists (including writers) and not-for-profit organizations in all creative fields.

Walter, Richard, Leslie Kallen Seminars, 15303 Ventura Blvd., #900, Sherman Oaks, CA 91403. 1-800-755-2785. Seminars.

Writer's Boot Camp, 1950 S. Pelham, #1, Los Angeles, CA 90025. (310) 268-2288. Six-week screenwriting course.

Writer's Center (Dr. Rachel Ballon), 1355 Westwood Blvd., Suite 204, Los Angeles, CA 90024. (310) 479-0048. Writers' psychotherapist/consultant who specializes in personal and career issues—works with both the writer and the writing.

Writers Workshop, P.O. Box 69799, Los Angeles, CA 90069. (213) 559-4512. Writer's organization. Workshops and contests.

Note: Most universities and colleges have continued-education departments that sponsor writing seminars, workshops, and non-credit courses.

PUBLICATIONS, DIRECTORIES, AND SUPPORT ORGANIZATIONS

Academy Players Directory, 8949 Wilshire Blvd., Beverly Hills, CA 90211. (310) 247-3000

The Big Screen Book, Suite 204, 137 N. Virgil Ave., Los Angeles, CA 90004. (213) 380-0472. Includes a section listing independent producers.

Blu-Book Directory. See *Hollywood Reporter*.

Creative Screenwriting, 518 Ninth St., N.E., Suite 308, Washington, DC 20002. Quarterly journal.

Daily Variety, 5700 Wilshire Blvd., Los Angeles, CA 90036. (213) 857-6600. The most-read trade publication. There is also a weekly version: *Weekly Variety*, same address, Suite 120. In New York: 249 W. 17th St., 4th Floor, New York, NY 10011.

Dramalogue, P.O. Box 38771, Hollywood, CA 90038. Weekly publication.

Hollywood Agents & Managers Directory, published by Hollywood Creative Directory, 3000 Olympic Blvd., Suite 2525, Santa Monica, CA 90404. (310) 315-4815. Other excellent directories are available. Can also be purchased at Samuel French Bookshops (see "Bookstores").

Hollywood Insiders: Low Budget Producers Directory, Hawkwind, Inc., 28924 S. Western, #107, San Pedro, CA 90732. Lists independent movie and TV producers.

The Hollywood Reporter, 5055 Wilshire Blvd., Los Angeles, CA 90036.
(213) 525-2000. Daily trade publication. Publishes the *Blu-Book Directory*, which lists names and companies involved in every aspect of film.

Hollywood Reporter Blu-Book Directory, published by *The Hollywood Reporter* (see "Bookstores"). They also publish a directory of participants of the American Film Market in February.

Hollywood Scriptwriter, 1626 N. Wilcox, #385, Hollywood, CA 90028.
(805) 495-5447. Excellent newsletter.

Interactive Directory, P.O. Box 10038, Marina del Rey, CA 90295. People and companies involved in the new technology.

International Interactive Communications Society, P.O. Box 6211, Malibu, CA 90264.
An organization for people in multimedia and interactive technology.

The Journal of the Writers Guild of America. Includes a section entitled "TV Market List," which lists current television shows that will read scripts. (See "Writer's Guild" under "Service Organizations and Unions.")

National Writers Association, 1450 S. Havana, Suite 424, Aurora, CO 80012.
(303) 751-7844. Provides reports, editing help, local chapters, and other services.

The New York Screenwriter, 545 8th Ave., Suite 401, New York, NY 10018.
(212) 967-7711, ext. 3165. Monthly publication for New York-based screenwriters.

Pacific Coast Studio Directory, P.O. Box V, Pine Mountain, CA 93222-4901. Studios, production companies, film commissions.

Premiere, published by Murdoch Magazines, 2 Park Ave., New York, NY 10016. Subscription at P.O. Box 55387, Boulder, CO 80323. (800) 289-2489. Available at any newsstand.

Scenario. Quarterly journal of screenplays. (800) 222-2654.

The Screenwriter's FORUM, P.O. Box 7, Long Green Pike, Baldwin, MD 21013.
(410) 592-3466. Screenwriting organization. Publishes *Script—the Magazine for the Entertainment Writer*. Feature, TV, cable, MOW, interactive, documentary, and DTV scriptwriting.

Screenwriter's Resource Guide, SunWest Media, 4 S. San Francisco St., #221, Flagstaff, AZ 86001. Directory of resources.

Scriptwriters Network, 11684 Ventura Blvd., #508, Studio City, CA 91604. Professional organization. Must submit a completed script to gain full membership.

Wisconsin Screenwriter's Forum, 221 Frigate Dr., Madison, WI 53705. Writers organization, newsletter, and contest.

Writer's Aide, 1685 S. Colorado Blvd., #237, Denver, CO 80222. (303) 430-4839. Complete information on screenwriting contests.

Writer's Connection, P.O. Box 24770, San Jose, CA 95154. (408) 445-3600. Newsletter and writers' organization. Sponsors seminars and the annual August "Selling to Hollywood" conference.

Writer's Digest, published by F&W Publications Inc., 1507 Dana Ave., Cincinnati, OH 45207. Monthly for writers in every medium. Available on any newsstand.

BOOKSTORES

Drama Book Shop, 723 Seventh Ave., 2nd Floor, New York, NY 10019. (212) 944-0591. New York's top film and drama bookstore.

Larry Edmunds Bookshop, 6644 Hollywood Blvd., Hollywood, CA 90028. (213) 463-3273. Industry books of every kind.

Limelight Bookstore, 1803 Market St., San Francisco, CA 94103. (415) 864-2265.

Samuel French Bookshop, 7623 Sunset Blvd., Hollywood, CA 90046. (213) 876-0570. Books and directories. They also have a location in the Valley—11963 Ventura Blvd., Studio City, CA 91604. (818) 762-0535. Mail order available. (800) 8-ACT NOW. FAX (213) 876-6822. E-mail: samfrench@earthlink.net. They carry everything for screenwriters, playwrights, and filmmakers.

The Write Stuff Catalog, 21115 Devonshire St., #182, Chatsworth, CA 91311. (818) 773-6460. Books for writers.

The Writer's Computer Store, 11317 Santa Monica Blvd., Los Angeles, CA 90025. (310) 479-7774. Your complete source for software and computers. Books also for sale. Catalog available. Mail-order available.

Note: Scripts may also be found in college libraries, the WGA offices, the Academy of Motion Picture Arts & Sciences, the American Film Institute, and the New York Public Library for the Performing Arts (40 Lincoln Center Plaza, New York, NY 10023).

SOFTWARE

AutoScript—Word processing and formatting programs for WordPerfect and Microsoft Word. Gemini Partners, P.O. Box 38410, Hollywood, CA 90038. (800) 299-6152.

The Character Construction Kit—Builds characters. The Screenwriter's FORUM, P.O. Box 7, Baldwin, MD 21013. (410) 592-3466.

Collaborator and *Collaborator II*—Story and character development. Collaborator Systems, Inc., P.O. Box 57557, Sherman Oaks, CA 91403. (800) 241-2655.

Corkboard—Organizes script ideas. MacToolKit, 1234 6th St., Suite 204, Santa Monica, CA 90401. (310) 395-4242.

Dramatica—Story development program. Screenplay Systems, 150 E. Olive Ave., Suite 203, Burbank, CA 91502. (818) 843-6557.

Final Draft for Macintosh—Word processing and formatting program. MacToolKit, 1234 6th St., Suite 204, Santa Monica, CA 90401. (310) 395-4242.

IdeaFisher—Idea creation and development. IdeaFisher Systems, Inc., 2222 Martin St., #110, Irvine, CA 92715. (800) 289-4332.

Macro Concepts—Add-on software for Microsoft Word for Macintosh and WordPerfect for DOS. Macro Concepts, P.O. Box 1534, Pacific Palisades, CA 90272.

Movie Master—Word processing and formatting program. Comprehensive Cinema Software, 148 Veterans Dr., Northvale, NJ 07647. (800) 526-0242.

PlayWrite, *ScreenWriter*, and *PlayWrite Pro*—Word-processing and formatting programs. PlayWrite Systems, P.O. Box 725, Sierra Madre, CA 91025-0725. (800) 62-PLAYS.

Plots Unlimited—Story-creation software. Ashleywilde, Inc., 23715 W. Malibu Rd., Suite 132. Malibu, CA 90265. (800) 833-PLOT.

Script Wizard—Add-on software for Microsoft Word for Windows. Stefani Warren & Associates, 1517 Hillside Dr., The Woodlands, Glendale, CA 91208. (818) 500-7081.

ScriptWright—Formatting program for Micosoft Word. Indelible Ink, 156 Fifth Ave., New York, NY 10010. (212) 255-1956.

Script Thing—Word processing. Script Thing, 3061 Massasoit Ave., San Diego, CA 92117. (619) 270-7515.

Scriptor—Formatting program. Screenplay Systems, 150 E. Olive Ave., Suite 203, Burbank, CA 91502. (818) 843-6557.

ScriptPerfection—Formatting program for WordPerfect. ScriptPerfection Enterprises, 3061 Massasoit Ave., San Diego, CA 92117. (619) 270-7515.

Scriptware—Word-processing and formatting program. Cinovation Inc., 1750 30th St., Suite 360, Boulder, CO 80301. (303) 786-7899.

Scriptwriting Tools—Add-on software for Microsoft Word. Morley & Associates, 120 East 94 1/2 Street, Bloomington, MN 55420. (612) 884-3991.

Story Vision—Screenwriting software for interactive media. Story Vision, 171 Pier Ave., Suite 204, Santa Monica, CA 90405. (310) 392-5090.

Storycraft—Fiction writing software. Storycraft Corporation, 820 W. 21st St., Suite 7, Norfolk, VA 23517. 1-800-97-STORY. (804) 623-1820.

Storyline Pro—Story creating and word processing. Truby's Writers Studio, 1737 Midvale Ave., Los Angeles, CA 90024. (800) 33-TRUBY.

WordScript —Formatting program for MacIntosh and Microsoft Word. Robert Arnold, 2232 Glenwood Ave., Toledo, OH 43620. (419) 242-2462.

WritePro—Sol Stein's fiction-writing program. The WritePro Corporation, 43 S. Highland Ave., Ossining, NY 10562. (800) 755-1124. Also offers *FictionMaster*.

Writer's Blocks for Windows—Organizes story ideas as in a step-outline. Ashley Software, 27758 Santa Margarita Parkway, Suite 302, Mission Viejo, CA. (714) 583-9153.

WriteWay—Helps you prepare and sell your script. The Write Way, P.O. Box 22517, St. Petersburg, FL 33742.

The Writer's Computer Store, 11317 Santa Monica Blvd., Los Angeles, CA 90025. (310) 479-7774. Your complete source for software and computers. Books also for sale. Catalog available. Mail-order available.

BOOKS FOR SREENWRITERS AND TELEVISION WRITERS

Adventures in the Screen Trade. William Goldman. Warner Books.
Alternative Scriptwriting: Writing Beyond the Rules. Ken Dancyger & Jeff Rush. Focal.
The Art of Adaptation. Linda Seger. Henry Holt.
The Art of Dramatic Writing. Lajos Egri. Simon & Schuster.
The Art of Screenwriting. William Packard. Paragon House.
Becoming a Writer. Dorothea Brande. J.P. Tarcher, Inc.
Comedy Writing Step by Step. Gene Perret. Samuel French Trade.
The Comic Toolbox. John Vorhaus. Silman-James Press.
The Complete Directory to Primetime Network TV Shows. Brooks and Marsh. Ballantine.
Corporate Screenwriting. Ray DeZazzo. Focal Press.
Creating Unforgettable Characters. Linda Seger. Henry Holt.
Dealmaking in the Film and Television Industry. Mark Litwak. Silman-James Press
The Elements of Screenwriting. Irwin R. Blacker.
Funny Business. Sol Saks. Lone Eagle Publishing.
Getting Your Script Through the Hollywood Maze, An Insider's Guide. Linda Stuart. Acrobat Books.
The Hero with a Thousand Faces. Joseph Campbell. Princeton University Press.
Hitchcock/Truffaut (Revised Edition). Francois Truffaut. Simon and Schuster.
How to Make It In Hollywood. Linda Buzzell. Harper Perennial.
How to Market, Promote, and Sell You and Your Project to the New Hollywood (Multimedia). Joyce A. Schwarz.
How to Sell Your Screenplay. Carl Sautter. New Chapter Press.
How to Write a Movie in 21 Days. Viki King. Harper & Row.
How to Write Plots that Sell. F.A. Rockwell. Contemporary Books.
How to Write for Television. Madeline DiMaggio. Simon & Schuster.
Making a Good Script Great—2nd Edition. Linda Seger. Samuel French Trade.
The New Screenwriter Looks at the New Screenwriter. William Froug. Silman-James Press.
On Writing Well. William Zinsser. Harper & Row.
Opening the Doors to Hollywood: How to Sell Your Idea. Carlos de Abreu & Howard Jay Smith. Custos Morum.
The Power of Myth. Joseph Campbell. Doubleday.
Reading for a Living. T.L. Katahn. Blue Arrow Books.
The Script Is Finished, Now What Do I Do? K Callan. Sweden Press.
Screenplay. Syd Field. Dell.
The Screenwriter Looks at the Screenwriter. William Froug. Silman-James Press.
Screenwriting: The Art, Craft and Business of Film and Television Writing. Richard Walter. New Am. Lib.

Screenwriting Tricks of the Trade. William Froug. Silman-James Press.
Selling a Screenplay. Syd Field. Dell.
Successful Script Writing. Wolff & Cox. Writer's Digest Books.
Successful Sitcom Writing. Jurgen Wolff. St. Martin's.
The Television Writer's Handbook. Constance Nash. Harper & Row.
The TV Scriptwriter's Handbook. Alfred Brenner. Silman-James Press.
TV Writing: From Concept to Contract. Richard A. Blum. Hastings House.
The Writer's Journey. Christopher Vogler. Michael Wiese Productions.
Writing & Selling Your Screenplay, Revised Edition. Four-tape audio program. David
    Trottier. The Screenwriting Center.
Writing for Television. Stuart M. Kaminsky. Dell.
Writing Screenplays that Sell. Michael Hauge. HarperCollins.
Writing Scripts Hollywood Will Love. Katherin Alwell Herbert. Allworth Press, New
    York.
Writing the Script. Wells Root. Holt, Rinehart & Winston.
You'll Never Eat Lunch in This Town Again. Julia Phillips. Penguin.

CONTESTS

Note: *Contest sponsors may change deadline dates, procedures, and other parameters.
Contact each for up-to-date information. Parameters change often. Although the
major contests are listed below, there are other, small contests sponsored by colleges, universities, film schools, and writing groups. These may be advertised in the
trades and other film and writing publications. Contact your state film commission
for information on local contests.*

America's Best Competition, The Writer's Foundation, 1801 Burnet Ave., Syracuse, NY
    13206. (315) 432-1235. Award: $25,000. Fee: $25-40, depending on category.
    Deadline: March.

Austin Heart of Texas Film Festival, 707 Rio Grande, #101, Austin, TX 78701. (512)
    478-4795, (800) 310-FEST. Award: $2,000. Fee: $25. Deadline: August.

The Chesterfield Program. See "Universal Studios/Chesterfield."

Christopher Columbus Society for the Creative Arts, 433 N. Camden Dr., Beverly Hills,
    CA 90210. (310) 288-1988. Award: $10,000 fellowship plus script development.
    Fee: $45. Deadline: Ongoing.

Conquest Media Screenplay Awards, Box 694, Huntsville, AL 35804. Award: $20,000
    for a one-year option. Fee: $49. Deadline: February 1. This is a new contest; in-
    vestigate carefully before submitting your script.

Diane Thomas Contest, UCLA Extension, 10995 Le Conte Ave., #313, Los Angeles, CA 90024-2883. Screenplay must be developed in a UCLA Writer's Program screenwriting class.

Disney Fellowship Program, Disney Studios, 500 S. Buena Vista St., Burbank, CA 91521-0880. Award: $30,000 year-long internship at Disney. WGA members not eligible. Program is open to all writers in motion picture and television, but gives preference to women and minorities. Deadline: April.

Hanover Square Production Contest, Hanover Square Productions, 1141 S. Robertson Blvd., Los Angeles, CA 90035. (310) 288-6326. Award: $20,000 for a six-month option. Fee: $30. Deadline: June 1.

Houston International Film Festival Contest, Worldfest/Houston (and Charleston), P.O. Box 56566, Houston, TX 77256. Award: Recognition and readings of your work by industry people. Fee: $80. Deadline: March 1.

Independent Filmmaker's Program, 6855 Santa Monica Blvd., Suite 207, Los Angeles, CA 90038. (213) 856-9136. Award: Possible opportunity for your screenplay to be produced; compensation. Fee: $50. No deadline. This is a new program; investigate carefully.

Malcolm-Vincent Screenwriting Contest, 505 S. Beverly Dr., Suite 17, Beverly Hills, CA 90212. Award: $5,000. Fee: $50. Deadline: Jan 31.

The New Harmony Project, 613 N. East St., Indianapolis, IN 46202. Award: Workshop with professional filmmakers. No fee. Deadline: Dec 1.

Nicholl Fellowship Competition, Academy of Motion Picture Arts and Sciences, 8949 Wilshire Blvd., Beverly Hills, CA 90211-1972. This is probably the most prestigious screenwriting competition. Entrant cannot have earned more than $1,000 as a screenwriter. Award: $25,000. Fee: $25. Deadline: First Monday in May.

Parkplace Productions' Screenwriting Competition, P.O. Box 48703, Doraville, GA 30362. Award: $2,500. Deadline: First week in July. Send SASE.

Pioneer Screenwriting Contest, Lightview Entertainment, 11901 Santa Monica Blvd., Suite 571, Santa Monica, CA 90025. $5,000 grant plus agency representation. Devoted to new writers of diverse backgrounds. $40 fee. Deadline: November 1.

Carl Sautter Memorial Scriptwriting Competition for Film and Television. The Scriptwriter's Network, 11684 Ventura Blvd., #508, Studio City, CA 91604. Competition for members only. Deadline: Mid-May. Fee: $30.

Screenwriter's FORUM Contests, P.O. Box 7, Long Green Pike, Baldwin, MD 21013. Award: Screenwriting products, exposure to agents. Deadline: Several contests a year are advertised in *Script* Magazine.

Sundance Institute, 225 Santa Monica Blvd., 8th Floor, Santa Monica, CA 90401. (310) 394-4662. Utah address: P.O. Box 16450, Salt Lake City, UT 84116. Conducts script development workshops in Utah each summer and winter. Only a few scripts are accepted. Run by Robert Redford. Fee: $25.

Universal Studios/Chesterfield Fellowship Contest, Chesterfield Film Company, Universal Studios, 100 Universal City Plaza, Building 447, Universal City, CA 91608. Award: Ten $20,000 year-long internships with the studio. Fee: $35. Deadline: Mid-May.

T.W. Wharton Screenwriting Awards, Odyssey Media, Box 4437, Ithaca, NY 14852. Award: $2,000. Deadline: Mid-February. Fee: $25.

Wisconsin Screenwriters Forum Contest, 221 Frigate Dr., Madison, WI 53705. Award: Recognition and feedback. Fee: $18 membership plus $18 processing fee. Deadline: October 1.

Writer's Digest Writing Competition, 1507 Dana Ave., Cincinnati, OH 45207. Award: $250. Fee: $5. Deadline: May 31.

Writer's Network Screenplay and Fiction Competition, 289 S. Robertson, Suite 465, Beverly Hills, CA 90211. (800) 64-NETWORK, (310) 843-9838. Award: $1000. Send SASE.

Writer's Aide, 1685 S. Colorado Blvd., #237, Denver, CO 80222. (303) 430-4839. Complete information on contests.

The Writers Workshop Contest, P.O. Box 69799, Los Angeles, CA 90069. (213) 933-9232. Award: Staged readings by industry leaders. (Minority contest winners also win $500—entrants must be African American, Latino, Asian, or Native American.) Fee: $65. Deadline: Ongoing.

CORRESPONDENCE COURSE

Imagine having your own individual tutor throughout the script development process! My script-development service provides critiques at the following phases to keep you on track and focused.

1 — Concept and core story
2 — Treatment
3 — Character development
4 — Step-outline
5 — First 30 pages
6 — Completed draft and query letter

Write at your own speed and pay as you go. Specific assignments guide you through every step of the writing process. I give you personal attention and adjust assignments to your needs. Call me or write for complete information.

SAVE $25 OFF THE REGISTRATION FEE BY TELLING ME YOU READ *THE SCREENWRITER'S BIBLE*!

SCRIPT EVALUATION AT REASONABLE RATES

$450 for a complete analysis by Dave Trottier. *Fee subject to change.* Evaluation includes six to twelve pages plus phone consultation. Just send your script with your check to The Screenwriting Center.

SAVE $50 ON YOUR SCRIPT EVALUATION BY TELLING ME YOU READ *THE SCREENWRITER'S BIBLE*!

Dave Trottier
The Screenwriting Center • *member, Forbes Communications Group*
869 East 4500 South, #100 • Salt Lake City, UT 84107
(801) 288-4150 • (800) 264-4900

General Index

Note: A complete formatting index appears on pages 101-103